D1567177

EXCURSIONS ALONG THE NILE:
The Photographic Discovery of Ancient Egypt

PLATE 13

EXCURSIONS ALONG THE NILE:
THE PHOTOGRAPHIC DISCOVERY OF ANCIENT EGYPT

Essay by Kathleen Stewart Howe

Santa Barbara Museum of Art
1993

Santa Barbara Museum of Art
1130 State Street
Santa Barbara, CA 93101

Travelers in an Antique Land: Early Travel Photography in Egypt
Exhibition Itinerary

Santa Barbara Museum of Art, Santa Barbara, California
February 19–April 24, 1994

The Baltimore Museum of Art, Baltimore, Maryland
July 19–October 1, 1995

The Nelson-Atkins Museum of Art, Kansas City, Missouri
October 20–December 3, 1996

Carleton University Art Gallery, Ottawa, Ontario, Canada
February 4–April 14, 1996

Editor: Patricia Ruth
Designer: Karen Bowers, Curatorial Assistance, Inc.
Publication Manager: Cathy Pollock

Printer: Pearl River Printing Company, Ltd.
Paper stock: New Age matte 157 gsm
Typefaces: Stone Serif, Americana

Photography: Curatorial Assistance, Inc., unless otherwise noted

Printed in Hong Kong

Library of Congress Cataloging-in-Publication Number 93-41648
Soft Cover ISBN 0-89951-089-2
Hard Cover ISBN 0-89951-088-4

OZYMANDIAS

I met a traveler from an antique land

Who said: Two vast and trunkless legs of stone

Stand in the desert. . . . Near them, on the sand,

Half sunk, a shattered visage lies, whose frown,

And wrinkled lip, and sneer of cold command,

Tell that its sculptor well those passions read

Which yet survive, stamped on these lifeless things,

The hand that mocked them, and the heart that fed:

And on the pedestal these words appear:

"My name is Ozymandias, King of Kings:

Look on my works, ye Mighty, and despair!"

Nothing beside remains. Round the decay

Of that colossal wreck, boundless and bare

The lone and level sands stretch far away.

—PERCY BYSSHE SHELLEY

AUTHOR'S
ACKNOWLEDGMENTS

This essay grew out of discussions with Michael Wilson about the connections between travelers, tourists, and photographs in Egypt in the nineteenth century. I owe him a great debt of gratitude for sharing his knowledge and the fruits of a collector's passion with me. I would also like to thank generous friends and colleagues for their assistance. In Paris, André Jammes, Gérard Lévy and François Lepage gave me the benefit of their scholarship and allowed me to examine photographs in their collections. Critical reading by Eugenia Parry Janis and Michele Penhall sharpened and strengthened the essay. Karen Sinsheimer and Cathy Pollock of the Santa Barbara Museum of Art were unfailingly helpful. Finally, I am particularly indebted to my husband who, once again, diplomatically combined tough critical standards with enthusiastic support. I gratefully acknowledge Nissan Perez, whose work established a foundation for all subsequent studies of photography in nineteenth-century Egypt.

CONTENTS

8

FOREWORD

Karen Sinsheimer

10

MAP OF 19TH-CENTURY EGYPT

11

EXCURSIONS ALONG THE NILE:
THE PHOTOGRAPHIC DISCOVERY OF ANCIENT EGYPT

Kathleen Stewart Howe

44

NOTES

47

SELECTED PLATES

154

APPENDIX A: CHRONOLOGY

156

APPENDIX B: PRINCIPAL BIOGRAPHIES

164

APPENDIX C: NOTES ON SELECTED PHOTOGRAPHS

Michael G. Wilson

170

SELECTED BIBLIOGRAPHY

172

INDEX

FOREWORD

No matter the century or era in which the adventurer seeks out Egypt, from Herodotus who journeyed to a world that was already ancient by the fifth century B.C., to the archaeologist in 1993 for whom new discoveries are still possible, Egypt continues to be seductive and evocative, full of mystery, promise, wonder, and, inevitably, new discovery.

Surveying the photographic imagery produced by dozens of nineteenth-century photographers of varying nationalities evokes that same sense of discovery and mystique. The exhibition of photographs entitled *Travelers in an Antique Land: Early Photography in Egypt,* featured in its entirety in this volume, leads the visual explorer through four decades of cultural and geographic history. It reveals, as does this book, how the perceptions and images of Egypt were shaped by the times as much as by the timelessness of the place. An examination of the photographic images of ancient Egypt that date from the 1840's reveals a new vantage point on an old subject. For, from the moment photography arrived on the scene (some forty years after Napoleon's arrival in 1798), photographers chronicled and reflected Egypt as it passed, in Peter Clayton's words, from "the age of the savant [to] the age of the tourist." The process took less than a century, and the photographer arrived in time to capture, in a way that no written account can, the transformation of a strange, almost mystical faraway land to a commonplace tour destination.

Memorialized by countless photographers (thirty of varying nationalities are represented in this publication and exhibition), the overall view is of ancient cultural landscape, forty-three centuries old, newly made familiar. The photographers, while faithfully documenting Egypt and/or their impressions of it, offer a sociological and historical as well as an aesthetic perspective on the "discovery" of Egypt.

The genesis of this exhibition and publication was a series of discussions with Michael G. Wilson, and the superb collection of nineteenth-century photographs that Michael and his wife Jane have amassed with great care and connoisseurship.

The Albert R. Broccoli Foundation provided generous support for a publication befitting the quality of the photographs. Graham Howe and his associates at Curatorial Assistance provided design and other expertise in the course of preparing the publication. Cathy Pollock, with her skill and efficiency, brought the project in on time and within budget. Sandy Lee and William Stern provided invaluable volunteer assistance in preparation of the biographical material.

I also wish to acknowledge many museum staff members, who, in addition to their professional skill, offered both helpful suggestions and enthusiasm for the project: Director Paul N. Perrot, Terry Atkinson and Jay Ewart, John Coplin and his crew, Barbara Luton, Lauren Silverson, and Shelley Ruston. Robert Henning, Assistant Director for Curatorial Services, offered support and encouragement throughout. Finally, it was a privilege to work with Kathleen Howe, author of the essay, whose knowledge and professionalism helped realize the quality the Museum sought to achieve.

— Karen Sinsheimer
Curator of Photography

EGYPT, 1854

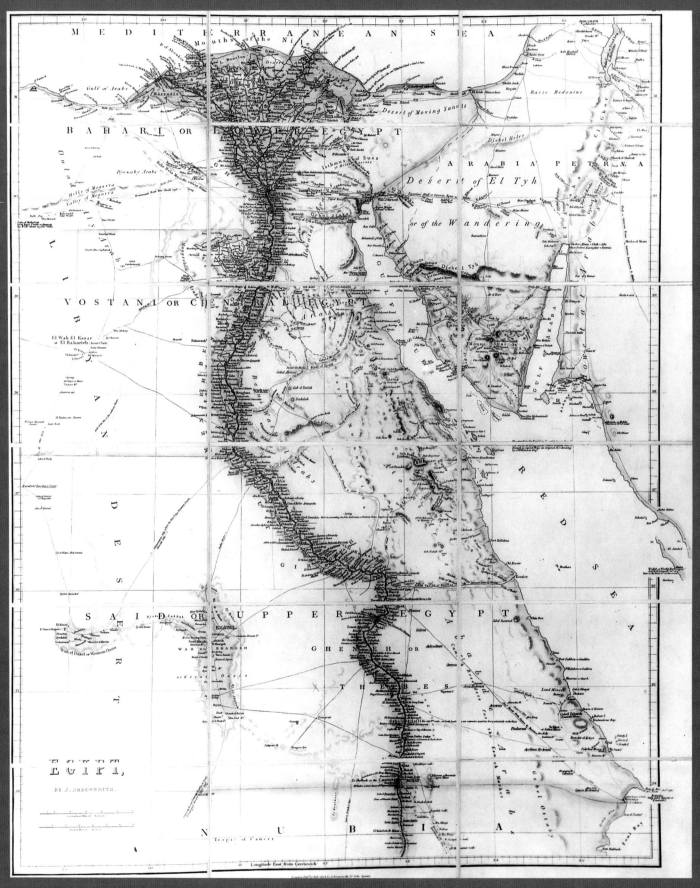

Map of nineteenth-century Egypt by John Arrowsmith, 1854.
Department of Special Collections, University Research Library, UCLA

EXCURSIONS ALONG THE NILE:
THE PHOTOGRAPHIC DISCOVERY OF ANCIENT EGYPT

Kathleen Stewart Howe

Journeys, those magic caskets full of dreamlike promises, will never again yield up their treasures untarnished. A proliferating and overexcited civilization has broken the silence of the seas once and for all. . . . I can understand the mad passion for travel books and their deceptiveness. They create the illusion of something which no longer exists but still should exist.

— Claude Levi-Strauss
Tristes Tropiques (1975)

Late in the hot afternoon of 21 July 1798, Napoleon stood before the French army, arrayed in battle formation on the plains of the West bank of the Nile, between the great pyramids at Giza and the village of Imbaba. The army stood waiting to engage the Mameluke force drawn up before them. Gesturing toward the heavy forms on the horizon, General Bonaparte invoked the pyramids as witness to French glory: "Soldiers, forty centuries look down upon you."[1] The Army of the Nile overwhelmed the Mamelukes; Cairo fell to the French, and Egypt was conquered.

Sixty-nine years later, an American tourist in Egypt, Mark Twain, had a rather different experience of the Pyramids to recount. He saw nothing but

a corrugated, unsightly mountain of stone. . . . Insect men and women were creeping about its dizzy perches and one little black swarm were waving postage stamps from the airy summit—handerkerchiefs will be understood.[2]

The Battle of the Pyramids and the tourist infestation of Cheops' "dizzy perches" in 1867 (p. 139) would seem to have little in common. Yet they are linked by the train of events set in motion when Napoleon decided to annex Egypt to France in 1798. The story of travelers and photography in nineteenth-century Egypt opens with Napoleon standing before the Pyramids, and encompasses the acquisition, exploration, spoliation, and consumption of Egypt during the nineteenth century.

Western travel to Egypt, which began with the great scientific expeditions initiated by Napoleon, evolved into the age of global tourism inaugurated by Thomas Cook. Egyptian travel generated hundreds of images which flowed from the pens of amateur sketchers and trained draughtsmen, until the invention of photography in 1839 placed a new method of making pictures at the traveler's service. In turn, photographic representations of Egypt encouraged more travelers and stimulated a demand for more images.

From our harried perspective in the late twentieth century, early photographs of Egypt seem to record a more leisurely and less complex life, where a traveler could while away an afternoon under a parasol working on a sketch of the Great Pyramid and Sphinx (p. 103). Today's students of Egypt return to the photographs made over one hundred years ago to study sites that have since disappeared and to catch a glimpse of the ancient river before it was transformed by man's intervention. We look through the camera's lens at things irretrievably altered by the passage of time. The palms of Philae, which was then known as the jewel of the Nile, may beckon to us from nineteenth-century photographs (p. 80), but, in fact, today the island, stripped of its temples, lies beneath Lake Nasser. Perhaps more importantly, the photographs chronicle attitudes as well as geography. Images of Egypt expose the preconceptions and values of the people who made and purchased them. Colonial attitudes determined the insistence by late nineteenth-century commercial photographers and their customers that Egyptians were quaintly costumed *types* who plied outlandish trades (p. 119). In turn, the photographic representation of types reinforced attitudes of cultural superiority because the photograph was perceived as documenting an objective reality. As both windows and mirrors, nineteenth-century photographs of Egypt record the transformation of a country and reflect the changing character of its visitors.

THE FATAL ATTRACTION OF EGYPT

The ultimate and unlikely result of the French desire to possess Egypt was an unparalleled boom in travel and tourism to Egypt in the second half of the nineteenth century. Egypt's attraction for Napoleon and for later visitors lay in their identification of it as a mythic locus of greatness. Writing ten years after the Battle of the Pyramids, Jean-Baptiste Fourier, a mathematician who had traveled with Napoleon as head of the Commission of Egypt, justified the invasion through just such an appeal to the past.

This country presents only great memories; it is the homeland of the arts and conserves innumerable monuments; its principal temples and the palaces inhabited by its kings still exist, even though its least ancient edifices had already been built by the time of the Trojan War. Homer, Lycurgus, Solon, Pythagoras, and Plato all went to Egypt to study the sciences, religion, and the laws. Alexander founded an opulent city there, which for a long time enjoyed commercial supremacy and which witnessed Pompey, Caesar, Mark Antony, and Augustus deciding between them the fate of Rome and that of the entire world. It is therefore proper for this country to attract the attention of illustrious princes who rule the destiny of nations.[3]

When he claimed the inevitability of Napoleon's interest, Fourier placed Egypt at the center of the ancient world and at the beginning of recorded history, recalling that it had also been a destination for Greek and Roman travelers whose written works were well known to his classically educated audience. (In fact, nineteenth-century travelers delighted in carving their names beneath the graffiti left by classical visitors, as seen in the upper left corner of fig. 1). Fourier's

Figure 1
Achille Constant Theodore Émile Prisse D'Avennes
Colosse de Ramses II à Wady Esseboua **(Colossus of Ramses II at Es-Sabua)**
Plate XX from *Monuments Égyptiens, bas reliefs, peintures, inscriptions, etc.*
Paris: Didot, 1847
Lithograph
Courtesy of the Trustees of the Public Library of the City of Boston

statement itself is almost a direct paraphrase of Diodorus Siculus, who in 58 B.C. wrote that "those men who have won the greatest repute in intellectual things have been eager to visit Egypt in order to acquaint themselves with its laws and institutions."[4] Thus, Egypt was claimed as the young general's destiny as the ordained leader and embodiment of French classical culture.

Although not part of the rhetoric, there were other reasons for the French occupation. Geopolitical strategy dictated that France deny her enemy England easy access to India, England's largest and richest colony, by holding the land route through Egypt. Domestic French politics also played a role. It was in the best interests of the French Directorate, as it struggled to consolidate power after the excesses of the Terror, to keep the popular young Napoleon as far from the volatile Parisian political scene as possible. Political and strategic considerations aside, Egypt carried an enormous weight of associations which were never far from the minds of members of the French Expedition. Michel-Ange Lancret, a civil engineer with the Army of the Nile, was well aware that his presence in Egypt placed him at the source of history, following the footsteps of classical antiquity. It was not coincidental that he chose to ride alone by moonlight to Philae, along the same causeway that the geographer Strabo had followed 2000 years earlier.

Night rides always have a grave and portentous quality that predisposes the mind to profound impressions. But what other place could produce stronger sensations or leave so many memories? I reflected with a mingling of excitement, pleasure, and apprehension that I was in one of the most extraordinary locations on the earth, amid places that partake of the fabulous, the very names of which, recited since childhood, have assumed gigantic and almost magical significance. I could touch the rocks of the cataracts of the gates of Ethiopia, at the boundary of the Roman Empire. Soon I would cross to that island where the tomb of Osiris had been, an island once sacred and now ignored, the sanctuary of an ancient religion, the mother of so many others. Finally, I was close to one of the immutable divisions of our globe (the Tropic of Cancer) and the step I had just taken might have carried me into the equatorial zone.[5]

THE DESCRIPTION DE L'ÉGYPTE

Napoleon's effort to secure Egypt as a French province ended in military disaster when Nelson destroyed the French fleet at Aboukir on 2 August 1798 and sealed the ultimate fate of the Army of the Nile. The Egyptian adventure was, however, a triumph for scholarship, because Napoleon's grandiose sense of the historic significance of the conquest of Egypt recast it in terms of the civilizing mission of France.[6] As Fourier stated, the action was motivated by a desire "to offer a useful European example to the Orient, and finally also to make the inhabitants' lives more pleasant and procure for them all the advantages of a perfect civilization."[7] To this end, Napoleon personally recruited a company of scholars to accompany the French Expeditionary Force. The 151 representatives from the arts and the applied and pure sciences were formally constituted as the Commission de l'Égypte after they landed at Alexandria.[8] Their mandate was simple: they were to investigate and document Egypt, modern and antique in its entirety.

The massive project of publishing the work of the Commission began under Emperor Napoleon in 1808 and ended in 1822, the year after his death as a prisoner on St. Helena. *Description de l'Égypte* consisted of ten large folio volumes of plates, three atlases, nine volumes of memoirs, descriptions and geographical surveys, and an introductory volume containing Fourier's "Historical Preface." Plates and commentary were divided between *The Modern State* and *Antiquities*. *Description de l'Égypte* defined Egypt for the next fifty years, a definition that carried the assumption that Egyptian antiquity belonged to the West rather than to modern Egyptians, by right of intellect. The illustrations in the *Description* repeatedly contrasted the scholarly activity of the French with the lethargy of the Arab inhabitants (fig. 2).

, VUE DE L'INTÉRIEUR DE LA GROTTE PRINCIPALE.
₂ VUE D'UNE ANCIENNE CARRIERE.

Figure 2

Antoine Cécile
El Kab (Elethyia), *Vue de l'interieur de la grotte principale* (Interior of the principal grotto at El Kab)
Plate 67 from vol. 1, *Description de l'Égypte*
Paris: Imprimerie impériale, 1809–1823
Engraving
From the Resource Collections of the Getty Center for the History of Art and the Humanities

Conceived in encyclopedic terms, entries in the *Description* surveyed the natural history and natural resources of the region, described the state of manufacturing, mining, and agriculture, depicted the social structure and religious customs of the people, and, of course, catalogued the antique remains. Its Brobdingnagian scope was matched by unusually large physical dimensions which required specially manufactured paper. The publisher offered a richly decorated library cabinet designed with an $8^1/2$- by 5-foot reading stand to hold the open volumes. This landmark of French scholarship, the result of the first systematic exploration of Egypt, had a direct impact on the photography of Egypt. One of the earliest exhaustive photographic surveys of Egypt was undertaken by Félix Teynard as a "complement to the great *Description de l'Égypte*" (pp. 55–61).

PILGRIMS AND ADVENTURERS

During the many centuries since Herodotus, Pliny, and Strabo had explored Egypt, Western visitors had been rare. The few Christian pilgrims visiting Biblical sites were actively discouraged after Islam claimed Egypt in 639 A.D. In 870 A.D., when Bernard the Wise and two companions tested the prohibition, they discovered the cost of official disapproval. Forbidden permission to come ashore, they bribed the ship's captain to land them along the coast. On their arrival in Cairo, they were imprisoned. Only another sizable bribe secured their release. They spent a few days in the vicinity of Cairo visiting the Great Pyramids (at the time identified as the granaries built by Joseph) before leaving for Jerusalem.

In 1250, the Mamelukes, a warrior caste drawn from freed Circassian slaves, gained control of Egypt. From 1516, when they swore fealty to the Ottoman Empire, until the French Expedition, they ruled as the Sultan's representative in Egypt. Purchased as children, converted to Islam, and trained as soldiers, they were freed by their owners when they demonstrated proficiency as warriors, and became part of his personal militia. Personal loyalty to the owners who had trained and freed them was the organizing principle of Mameluke society. In theory, Mameluke society was a warrior meritocracy and power was not hereditary. In practice, the human desire to secure the position of one's children led to factional fighting and conflicts over succession.

Travel in Egypt was difficult and dangerous, but there will always be a few adventurers for whom the attraction of a journey lies in the challenge it presents. Pietro Della Valle, the son of a noble Roman family, undertook an extensive journey through Egypt, India, and Persia in the early 1600's and chronicled his travels in a series of letters to a scholar friend for eventual publication.[9] Even though Della Valle had secured safe passage from the Sultan in Constantinople, he faced innumerable difficulties in securing local permission for his movements and found little official protection from bandits and thieves. The dangers he reported were not likely to induce large numbers to follow in his footsteps. However, Della Valle's activities in Egypt were a harbinger of future Western depredations. He ransacked tombs at Thebes for mummy fragments, which apothecaries dissolved in liquid to prepare *momiya*, regarded as a potent medicine. Swallowing the loathsome draft seems suitable punishment for the wanton vandalism inherent in its preparation.

By the first part of the eighteenth century, the major European powers had established diplomatic ties with the Ottoman Empire. More Europeans made their way to Egypt, usually in connection with diplomatic or commercial interests, although, later in the century, gentlemen scholars extended their Grand Tour to include the Holy Land and Egypt. Their accounts joined the flood of travel books, which had become a hugely popular literary form. The objects with which they returned fed a general antiquarian passion for the old and curious. Neither systematically collected nor considered works of art, these antiquities found their way into the eclectically organized *wunderkammer* or cabinet of curiosities which almost every educated person seemed compelled to assemble.[10] Thus, an alabaster statue of Horus, looted from a tomb and sold in a Cairo bazaar, might join a hodgepodge of objects: fossils, preserved anatomical specimens, Roman coins, shells, oddly shaped roots, crystals, and the purported remains of fantastic animals.

Three years after Napoleon's Army of the Nile defeated the Mamelukes at the Battle of the Pyramids, they were ousted by the British, who returned titular control of Egypt to the Ottoman Sultan in 1802. In the ensuing struggle for local control of Egypt, Mohammad-Ali, an Albanian Bey in the Turkish Army, led a successful military revolt against the weakened Mamelukes, who were trying to reestablish control. Mohammad-Ali began a line of succession which ended with King Farouk in 1952.

The painful lesson of Egypt's vulnerability to European forces was not lost on Mohammed-Ali. After he consolidated his rule in 1811 by massacring the remaining Mamelukes, he embarked on an ambitious program of modernization. The number of Europeans and their position in Egypt expanded dramatically as a result of Mohammed-Ali's Westernization campaign. He hired French engineers, military advisors, and physicians whose presence can be deduced not only from the modern structures built under their direction, such as the Nile Barrage (p. 101), but from the stream of information about Egypt that began to reach Europe. Throughout the rest of the century, because of the debts incurred by Mohammad-Ali and his successors in their drive to transform Egypt, the country was a de facto client state of the French, initially, and then of the British. For the first time in centuries, Western travelers could move at will throughout the country.

Not only did the number of visitors swell dramatically after 1800, but their itineraries, once in Egypt, expanded. Guided by the detailed descriptions in travel accounts published by members of the Commission of Egypt and the first accurate maps drawn by the French military, they ventured beyond the region around Cairo.

Baron Dominique Vivant Denon's *Voyage dans la Basse et la Haute Égypte* (1802) was by far the most popular book about the Egyptian Expedition. An aide to Napoleon, Denon, rode south into Upper Egypt with General Desaix's division in pursuit of retreating Mamelukes. Denon's real quarry, however, was the ancient sites along the army's route. "If a fondness for antiquities has frequently made me a soldier, on the other hand, the kindness of soldiers, in aiding my researches, has often made antiquarians of them."[11] He recorded the contributions of his military companions in the drawings he made of the ruins (fig. 3). Denon was an engaging storyteller and a gifted illustrator. His tales of long rides and desolate ruins measured by exhausted soldiers, accompanied by sketches made from horseback, whetted the appetite for Egyptian travel. Translated into English and German almost immediately, *Voyage* was a best-seller, with at least forty editions appearing by 1885.

THE RAPE OF THE NILE[12]

Egyptian artifacts now poured into Europe, collected by scholars and adventurers alike. Henry Salt and Bernardo Drovetti, respectively the British and French consuls in Cairo, waged a fierce contest over the choicest items for themselves and their governments. Ironically, Salt sold his first collection to the Louvre and Drovetti's finds formed the nucleus of the first museum dedicated to Egyptian antiquities which was founded at Turin. Visitors felt compelled to bring something back from Egypt and the journey became a mad grab for ever more spectacular finds. The rhetoric of thievery justified plunder as a right conferred by cultural superiority. As Captain de Verminac Saint-Maur, commander of the 1830 French expedition which removed the obelisk from Luxor to its current site in Paris at the Place de Concorde, proclaimed: "Antiquity is a garden that belongs by natural right to those who cultivate and harvest its fruits."[13]

Vue d'un temple de Thèbes à Kournou .

Figure 3

Baron Dominique Vivant Denon
***Vue d'un temple de Thèbes à Kournou* (Temple at Thebes, Karnak)**
Plate 41 from *Voyage dans la Basse et la Haute Égypte*, 1802
Engraving
From the Resource Collections of the Getty Center for the History of Art and the Humanities

The plundered artifacts enthralled audiences, who were seduced by tales of discovery and acquisition. No one told a better story than Giovanni Belzoni, who had been known as the Patagonian Giant during a career as a carnival strongman. Belzoni was a self-styled hydraulic engineer who went to Egypt to sell Mohammad-Ali an improved waterwheel of his own invention. When his prototype failed disastrously, the British Consul-General Henry Salt hired Belzoni to secure the colossal granite head of Ramses II, which lay half-buried in the sand at Thebes. In his first outing as an antiquities collector, the strongman organized a crew to move the massive sculpture to the river bank, where it was loaded on a small boat for the trip to Cairo. Shipped to London and displayed in the British Museum, the Patagonian Giant's trophy became the catalyst for one of the great Romantic sonnets. Mesmerized by the coldly beautiful young king, Percy Bysshe Shelley wrote "Ozymandias." In the next few years, Belzoni discovered the tomb of Seti I, opened the passage into the Pyramid of Chephren, and dug his way into the temple at Abu Simbel. The 1820 publication of his lively adventures and the exhibition of finds and drawings which he mounted in London were potent stimuli to British Egyptomania.[14]

"AWFUL RUINS"

This, then, was the situation when Victor Hugo, the most influential French literary figure of his time, composed the long prose poem "Les Orientales" (1829). Studied and collected, the locus of history and a source of sensual delight, Egypt had invaded the Western psyche. In the preface to "Les Orientales," Hugo proclaimed the Orient, as the lands east of Europe were called, the pre-eminent object of intellectual endeavor and subject of Romantic musing:

> Today for a thousand reasons, all of which foster progress, the Orient is of more concern than it has ever been before. Never before have oriental studies been explored so deeply. In the century of Louis XIV one was a Hellenist: today one is an Orientalist. . . . Today we have a scholar assigned to every Oriental idiom from China to Egypt. As a result of this, the Orient—as an image or as an idea—has become for the intellect as well as the imagination a sort of general preoccupation, to which the author of this book has succumbed, perhaps without realizing.[15]

If Egypt intrigued the scholar, it inflamed the imagination of the Romantic. Romanticism was a reaction against the formal, rational, and measured canons of taste and conduct derived from classical antiquity. Romantics sought heightened emotional states elicited by wild feelings of terror, savored in languorous states of passion, or found in reveries of lost glory, the inexorable passage of time, and doomed love. The Egypt of Romantic imagination was a place where melancholic ruins of an ancient past brooded over scenes of barbaric Mameluke splendor; where cruelly sensual Pashas reigned over submissive harems, and noble Bedouin tribes traversed the limitless sands of the desert. The Romantic vision of Egypt preoccupied artists, many of whom traveled there (fig. 4).[16] This sensual dream of

Egypt, fueled by the poetry of Hugo and Byron, suffused with the intense colors, sharp odors, and exotic melodies of the Arabian Nights[17], caused young Gustave Flaubert to exclaim, "Oh, how willingly I would give up all the women in the world to possess for one night the mummy of Cleopatra!"[18]

A more contemplative mode of Romanticism was attracted to the "awful" ancient debris along the Nile that recalled the fearful transience of man. These same ruins were by now also associated with lost Napoleonic glory, a touchstone for young Frenchmen disgusted with the avaricious regime of the Citizen-King Louis Philippe. Among the British, Shelley turned to the Nile as the setting for the heightened emotional state that characterized Romantic solitude. As described by the poet in "Alastor; Or, the Spirit of Solitude," the intense experience of solitude is the deepest source of poetic inspiration:

His wandering step
Obedient to high thoughts, has visited
The awful ruins of days of old: . . .
the eternal pyramids,
Memphis and Thebes. . . .
Among the ruined temples there,
Stupendous columns, and wild images
Of more than man, where marble daemon watch
The Zodiac's brazen mystery, and dead men
Hang their mute thoughts on the mute walls around,
He lingered, poring on memorials
Of the world's youth, through the long burning day
Gazed on those speechless shapes, nor, when the moon
Filled the mysterious halls with floating shades
Suspended he that task, but ever gazed
And gazed, till meaning on his vacant mind
Flashed like strong inspiration, and he saw
The thrilling secrets of the birth of time.[19]

Many of the earliest practitioners of photography in Egypt were imbued with this strand of Romanticism. In the early calotypes of the ruins along the Nile by Félix Teynard, J. B. Greene, and Louis De Clercq, photographic representation is fused with a melancholy meditation on the passage of time. The inherent qualities of the calotype, a salted paper print made from a paper negative, found their fullest expression in the brooding images summoned by a

Romantic sensibility. The paper of the calotype negative absorbed the photographic chemicals which dispersed along its microscopic fibers. Light entering the camera infiltrated this sensitized paper, weaving an image into the fabric of the paper. In the calotype, ancient sites sank into the nap of the paper, revealed with a softness and delicacy of shadow and detail that creates an atmosphere of dreamlike stasis. J. B. Greene's calotypes of the hypostyle hall at Karnak and the statue of a woman at Abu Simbel (pp. 63, 65) are part apparition from the past, part record of the present. The *Interior Colonnade at Edfu* by Louis De Clercq becomes a profound meditation on time's dimensions (p. 98). The slow accumulation of sand over the long passage of archaeological time inexorably drifts into the temple colonnade which stands as stubborn witness to its own historical moment. The insubstantial figures seated in this ancient place speak eloquently of the transitory nature of individual human life, while the sun's movement across the sky, revealed in the blurred edges of the shadows, ticks off the minutes of the photographer's exposure.[20]

Figure 4
Baron Antoine-Jean Gros
Chef de Mamelucks à cheval
(Mounted Mameluke Chieftain), 1817
Lithograph 32.3 x 23.3cm
Gift of the Friends of Art, University Art Museum,
University of New Mexico, Albuquerque, New Mexico

CRACKING THE HIEROGLYPHIC CODE

Egypt was transformed from a curiosity to a scholarly discipline by the systematic cataloguing and mapping of sites by the Commission of Egypt (fig. 5). Nevertheless, the pursuit of scholarly enquiry promoted by the exquisitely detailed engravings in *Description de l'Égypte* was stymied because the hieroglyphs on the monuments so catalogued remained indecipherable. Indirectly, the French military campaign yielded the solution when soldiers digging fortifications near the Delta town of Rosetta uncovered a carved tablet. The rough slab of basalt carried a proclamation written in three scripts, hieroglyphic, a late cursive Egyptian script called demotic, and Greek. The spirit of intellectual inquiry fostered by Napoleon evidently extended to line officers, because Lt. François-Xavier Bouchard suspected the stone's significance and had it sent to the Commission in Cairo where it arrived in August 1799. It became a British spoil of war when the French surrendered Egypt in 1801. Moved to its new home in the British Museum, the Rosetta Stone tantalized philologists and engaged puzzle-lovers of all sorts. Although the riddle of hieroglyphic writing remained unsolved for twenty years, the Rosetta Stone's existence promised an eventual solution and inspired the collection of hieroglyphic texts.

Jean-François Champollion's breakthrough in hieroglyphic decipherment in 1822 initiated the formal study of Egyptian antiquity.[21] In relatively short order dates and dynastic lists were translated. Scholars rushed to construct the history of a past of even greater antiquity than they had suspected. Although the ability to decipher inscriptions gave impetus to their collection, the labor of copying the inscriptions that seemed to cover every surface was overwhelming. Napoleon's scholars had wavered before the task and filled their beautifully detailed drawings with approximations and interpolations. Nevertheless, it was becoming increasingly apparent that the inscriptions of Egypt had somehow to be recorded soon, before treasure-hunting travelers wiped out the history of the Pharaohs.

CAMERAS AT THE PYRAMIDS

The first connection between photography and Egypt was made on 3 July 1839 when François Arago, Permanent Secretary of the Academy of Sciences, informed the French Chamber of Deputies of a remarkable invention by Louis-Jacques Mandé Daguerre, which produced a finely detailed photographic image on a polished metal plate. Arago, who had himself contributed to the debate on hieroglyphic decipherment, formally proposed the application of the daguerreotype to the study of Egypt and repeated his proposal to the heavily attended August joint session of the Academies of Sciences and Fine Arts where Daguerre's process was demonstrated.

> While these pictures are exhibited to you, everyone will imagine the extraordinary advantages which could have been derived from so exact and rapid a means of reproduction during the expedition to Egypt; everybody will realize that had we had this process in 1798 we would possess today faithful pictorial records of that which the learned world is forever deprived of by the greed of the Arabs and the

vandalism of certain travelers. . . . To copy the millions and millions of hieroglyphs covering only the exterior of the great monuments of Thebes, Memphis, Karnak, twenty years and scores of draughtsmen would be required. With the daguerreotype, a single man could execute this immense task . . . and the new images would surpass in fidelity and local color the work of our most skilled artists.[22]

Three months after Daguerre's process was disclosed, the Orientalist painter Horace Vernet, accompanied by his pupil Frédéric Goupil-Fesquet and his nephew Charles Bouton, arrived in Cairo with a daguerrean apparatus. Goupil-Fesquet described the group as "daguerreotyping like lions."[23] Coincidentally, Pierre Joly de Lotbinière, a Swiss citizen who had been in Paris when the August announcement was made, was staying at the same hotel. He

A. Vol. III.   THEBES. KARNAK.   Pl. 19.

VUE DU PALAIS PRISE DE L'INTÉRIEUR DE LA COUR.

Figure 5

Antoine Cécile
Thèbes, Karnak, Vue du palais prise de l'interieur de la cour
(View of the palace at Thebes, Karnak, taken from the interior court)
Plate 19 from vol. 3, *Description de l'Égypte*
Paris: Imprimerie impériale, 1809–1823
Engraving
From the Resource Collections of the Getty Center for the History of Art and the Humanities

too was busily making daguerreotypes.[24] Joly and the others seem to have joined forces, often photographing the same sites together: Goupil-Fesquet related that he and Joly postponed their dinner so that they could develop their plates and judge the success of their efforts at Gizah.[25]

Because each daguerreotype exposure resulted in a single, direct photographic positive, the public saw the first photographic images of Egypt either as impressions pulled from engraved daguerreotype plates or as aquatints based on daguerreotypes. The views made by Goupil-Fesquet, who seems to have been the photographer in the Vernet group, were pulled from engraved daguerreotype plates and included in Nicolas Lerebour's multivolume *Excursions Daguerriennes, representant les vues et les monuments les plus remarquables du globe* (1840–44). Joly's daguerreotypes were the basis for the aquatints in *Panorama d'Égypte et de Nubie* by Hector Horeau (1841).

Goupil-Fesquet's party worked in the area around Cairo for a few weeks and then continued on to Palestine. The distinction of being the first to sail up the Nile in order to make photographs belongs to Joly. A daguerreotype by Joly was the basis for this aquatint view of Medinet-Habu (fig. 6). J. B. Greene and Félix Teynard would photograph the same courtyard in the 1850's.

The first daguerreotypists in Egypt did not answer Arago's call for precise records of hieroglyphic inscriptions. Rather, the first photographic images of Egypt were architectural, a choice influenced by the avid market for travel views. The static mass of architecture was well suited to early daguerreotypes which required long exposure times but which could reproduce every masonry course and architectural detail in perfect perspective. Daguerreotypes of architectural monuments were miniature worlds collected thousands of miles away, fairy tale worlds that vanished and reappeared with the angle of light on the polished metal daguerreotype plates.

The early nineteenth-century market for travel views had been transformed and expanded by Baron Isidore Taylor's *Voyages pittoresques et romantiques dans l'ancienne France* (1820–78). The twenty volumes of *Voyages pittoresques,* in which the architectural remains of historic France were described and illustrated with thousands of lithographs by scores of artists, had an enormous impact on the early practice of photography.[26] The taste for ruins, the development of an archaeological interest in the past, and the illustrative techniques which prioritized emotional response over topographic clarity found their first coherent expression here and provided a model for early photographically illustrated travel books. *Voyages pittoresques,* which blended Romantic reverie and careful scholarship, stands in clear distinction to the measured clarity and scholarly diction of the *Description de l'Égypte.*

Since Arago's vision of photography in the service of Egyptian philological studies was not realized by the daguerreotypists, it remained for a rival photographic process, also unveiled in 1839, to wed hieroglyphic study to photographic image. By mid-1839, while Daguerre negotiated with the French government for compensation for the rights to his process, two other inventors, a wealthy English amateur and a French civil servant, had separately arrived at a different type of photographic process. Sometime in 1834, William Henry Fox Talbot began experimenting with a photographic process that yielded a paper positive. Dissatisfied with that approach, Talbot began thinking in

Figure 6
Hector Horeau
Medinet-Habu
Plate 18 from *Panorama d'Égypte et de Nubie*
Paris: Horeau, 1841
Aquatint from daguerreotype by Pierre Joly de Lotbinière
From the Resource Collections of the Getty Center for the History of Art and the Humanities

terms of a reversed image which could be used to make multiple copies, and, in August of 1835, Talbot made the first photographic negative on paper.[27] In France, Hippolyte Bayard arrived at a very similar process early in 1839 and mounted the first public exhibition of photographs on Bastille Day of that year.[28]

In the calotype process, as Talbot ultimately named it, a paper negative was exposed in the camera, developed, and used to print multiple paper photographs. In 1846, William Henry Fox Talbot used his paper negative process to reproduce a hieroglyphic text in a publication by Samuel Birch, the British Museum's expert in Egyptian papyri. The *Talbotype Applied to Hieroglyphics* (London, August 1846) was the first use of photography to provide multiple, precise copies of a hieroglyphic text for study.

Making a calotype was not simple but it was easier to manage in the field than the delicate and dangerous process of exposing daguerreotype plates to mercury fumes. Further refinements of Bayard's and Talbot's processes resulted in techniques adapted to the rigors of travel. The most popular was a dry waxed paper negative process, developed and taught by Gustave Le Gray, that allowed negatives to be prepared ahead of time and developed later.[29]

THE CALOTYPE IN EGYPT

The first great photographic records of Egypt were produced by three calotypists. The first arrived in Egypt in 1849: Maxime Du Camp, accompanied by the then equally unknown Gustave Flaubert, held a commission from the Ministry of Public Education to photograph the monuments of Egypt.[30] The twenty-seven-year-old Du Camp is an excellent example of the type of educated traveler making his or her way to Egypt at mid-century. A scholarly interest in Egyptology and Arabic literature had led him to join the Société Orientale in 1846. He enjoyed a slight reputation as a traveler in the Romantic tradition after the publication of *Souvenirs et paysages d'Orient* (Paris, 1848), an account of his travels in North Africa. The East had interested him for some time, but his engagement with photography was more recent. Du Camp learned to make photographs from Gustave Le Gray for the purpose of attracting government support for a lengthy journey through Egypt, Nubia, Syria, and Palestine. (Le Gray taught Du Camp, Greene, and Teynard. Ironically, although Le Gray also ended up in Egypt at the end of his career, his Egyptian photographs do not equal the attainments of his young disciples [p. 100].)

Du Camp's scholarly interests seem reason enough for his planned journey, but other factors, primarily literary, influenced him. In his memoirs, Du Camp recalled reading Victor Hugo's "Les Orientales" as a schoolboy. He was not alone: twenty years later, a new generation of writers and artists responded to Hugo's cult of the Romantic East. The literary inspiration Du Camp and Flaubert sought in the East was tied to the Romantic search for sensual experience. As Flaubert's letters and journals divulge, once the two young men were free of the inhibiting presence of family and society, they immersed themselves in a search for exotic pleasures.[31] Egypt and the Orient signified freedom from the constraints of European social norms, as Alexander Kinglake, setting out from Cambridge in 1834 for the East, had affirmed:

> It is sweet to find oneself free from the stale civilization of Europe . . . and so remembering how many poor devils are living in a state of utter respectability, you will glory the more in your own delightful escape.[32]

Whatever his motives for traveling to Egypt, Du Camp doggedly applied himself to the difficult task of making photographs. For some reason, he was unsuccessful with Le Gray's dry waxed paper process and turned to a wet paper technique learned from a fellow traveler. (The cause of Du Camp's failure with Le Gray's technique is a mystery: both Teynard and Greene appear to have used it successfully.) Bemused by Du Camp's singleminded pursuit of his task, Flaubert wrote to his mother on April 15: "I don't know how Max hasn't cracked up with this rage for photography which consumes him."[33] Writing years later, Du Camp recalled the effort that the work had cost:

> Photography wasn't then what it has become today. . . . The wet paper process was long, meticulous and required great skill and more than forty minutes to produce a finished negative. . . . Doing

photography was nothing compared to the real difficulty of transporting the amount of equipment, which was all glass, crystal and porcelain, on muleback, camel, or with the help of servants. I lived in a fever of activity, dreaming only of palm trees, the desert and ruined temples.[34]

In Beirut at the conclusion of his journey and after months of struggling with camera and chemical solutions, Du Camp traded his photographic equipment for several yards of embroidered fabric with which to decorate an Oriental bed in his Paris apartment. He never picked up a camera again.

Du Camp returned to Paris in May 1851 with 214 successful negatives.[35] One hundred and twenty-five of them, printed by Blanquart-Évrard and accompanied by Du Camp's text, were published in 1852 as *Égypte, Nubie, Palestine et Syrie: dessins photographiques recuillis pendant les années 1849, 1850 et 1851, accompagnés d'un texte explicatif,* the first book about Egypt to be completely illustrated with photographs (pp. 49–53). Du Camp's photographs of archaeological monuments were intended to be precise scientific records. Many were made in response to the French Academy of Inscriptions' request for records of specific inscriptions, such as that in the Great Temple at Philae (p. 51).

Archaeological sites comprise most of the ninety-four images of Egypt in the book, although Du Camp had made many photographs of Arab villages. The publisher insisted that views of ancient Egypt were of more interest to readers and rejected the Egypt of its current inhabitants.[36] This, as well as other early photographic surveys, slighted contemporary Egypt except as a source for piquant details, because, as the author of an 1856 travel book stated, "it is not that world we are seeking on Egyptian soil."[37]

On 16 December 1851, the second of the early calotypists received a passport from Monsieur Belin, the French Consul in Cairo, to travel in upper Egypt with his interpreter Abdalah and his servant Ali.[38] At thirty-four, Félix Teynard, a well-to-do young man from Grenoble, set out on a journey of personal exploration. He described the photographs he made of modest, modern buildings and imposing antiquities as "souvenirs" that registered his "sensations." In the accompanying text, the personal quality of his photographs is underscored by his insistence on the sense of solitude experienced by a lone European in the midst of a native population.[39] The 160 salted paper prints from Teynard's journey up the Nile were lavishly published in *Égypte et Nubie* (1854–58), which was described by Teynard as a photographic "complement" to the great *Description de l'Égypte* (pp. 55–61). It is not surprising that Teynard, a civil engineer from the provincial capital that had been home to the pioneering Egyptologist Champollion and to Fourier, the first editor of the *Description de l'Égypte* quoted at the beginning of this essay, would conceive of a photographic catalogue of ancient and modern Egypt in terms of the *Description.*

Teynard's photographs recapitulate his experience of Egypt. Through his images, we approach the caravan encampment at Korosko (p. 56), and pick our way through clumps of coarse desert grasses at Karnak (p. 55). Teynard, more than any other of the early photographers, harnessed the effects of light playing over ancient ruined faces to create photographs that still have an emotional resonance today (p. 61).

The third calotypist in this Egyptian processional was the American John Beasely Greene, a well-connected young man whose family operated a bank in Paris. Greene was something of a prodigy: by the age of eighteen he was a full member of two learned societies devoted to Egypt and the East, the Société Asiatique and the Société Orientale. He was also a founding member of the French Photographic Society. Greene's dual interests in Egyptology and photography uniquely qualified him to be the first practicing archaeologist to use photography. On his first trip to Egypt in 1853, Greene the scholar made careful documentary photographs of the monuments and inscriptions, while Greene the photographic artist who had studied with Gustave Le Gray, the great photographer of the Forest of Fontainebleau, made beautiful atmospheric studies of the Egyptian landscape (pp. 63–67). He distinguished between the two sides of his photographic practice, maintaining one file for the monuments and inscriptions and another for the landscape studies.

After a brief return to Paris, during which he deposited a set of prints with the Académie des Inscriptions et Belles-lettres and was persuaded by Blanquart-Évrard to allow some of his photographs to be published as *Le Nil* (1854), he returned to Egypt and obtained a *firman* or permit to conduct his own excavations at Medinet-Habu. At the end of the season, Greene once again returned to Paris, where he wrote a monograph describing the results of his excavation. Again Greene presented the results of his work to the Académie—a copy of the published monograph and a set of twelve photographs which documented the excavation. These twelve calotypes mark the first time that photography was used to record an archaeological dig.

In late 1855 he set off again, stopping in Algeria to photograph the excavation of a tomb. He continued on to Egypt, where death ended his journey in November 1856; he was twenty-four years old. His friend, the Egyptologist Théodule Dévéria, wrote to a mutual friend: "He [Greene] left here already seriously ill, but, however, in a state which allowed some hope that he would recover his health in a climate which already once before had cured him."[40] If concern for his health prompted Greene's travels, he was but one of many nineteenth-century sufferers of tuberculosis who sought an elusive recovery in the dry air and warm sun of Egypt.

The scope of the work completed by Du Camp, Teynard, and Greene was unique, but they were by no means the only calotypists in Egypt at the time. A few Nile travelers, some known to us by name, such as Lieutenant Wheelhouse, George Bridges, and John Shaw Smith, and others lost behind the title "Anonymous," made photographs as a personal record of their tour in the same way that earlier travelers had included sketches in their journals (pp. 69, 70).

There was a significant population of Europeans in Egypt at mid-century, either working for Mohammad-Ali's government or pursuing private commercial interests, and a few were amateur photographers. The photographs of these resident amateurs acknowledge contemporary Egypt and record the flow of life in Egypt. When Mohammed-Ali's chief engineer Robert Murray set up his camera, he chose to photograph Bulak, Cairo's port quarter (p. 68), rather than the street in the European quarter favored by visiting photographers (pp. 70, 71, 89). A later photograph attributed to Murray records a highly prized Arabian horse belonging to him or to a friend (p. 151).

Only a few of the early calotypists, perhaps inspired by the new disciplines of ethnography and anthropology, photographed the people of the region. Ernest Benecke, on an extensive tour of the Mediterranean and the Middle East in the early 1850's, made calotypes which include some of the earliest photographs of the people of the region (p. 54). The range of people Benecke was able to photograph, from slaves to sheiks, is unusual. Because of religious prohibitions against images, the subjects in later photographs of Egyptian people were often the most marginal members of society, prostitutes or beggars. Although little is known about him, Benecke's ability to establish a rapport that would induce Sheik Mokba and members of his group to pose for a photograph is remarkable.

The inhabitants of Nubia and the Sudan fascinated the architect Pierre Tremaux, who was engaged in an extensive survey of the architecture of Asia Minor and North Africa (p. 62). In a curious way, Tremaux's indifferent technical abilities lend a strange power to the photographs he made of the desert people along the upper Nile. The enigmatic figures seem veiled, their ancient way of life obscure, closed to Western examination. Ultimately, their nebulous photographic presence becomes a metaphor for their lack of substance in the calculations of the colonial powers.

No matter how poetically Egypt was recreated or how romanticized its people were, the underlying reality was that Europeans viewed the people of the region as specimens. The inhabitants of Egypt are the subject of only one of Félix Teynard's 160 photographs (p. 59). The helmsman and sailor from Aswan are not named individuals but representative members of a race which Teynard typed as "alert, vigorous, and very superior to the inhabitants of Lower Egypt, a degenerate race."[41] In Maxime Du Camp's photographs, his boatman functions as a human measuring rod to establish scale rather than as an individual presence (pp. 49, 50, 52).

In a nice bit of zoologic diplomacy, Halem Pasha, the Viceroy's brother, presented a young female hippopotamus to Napoleon III. It was accompanied to Paris by two Nubians who had cared for it since its capture. When Louis Rousseau photographed the animal at the Museum of Natural History, he made three photographs, one of the hippopotamus and one of each of the two Nubians (p. 152). The photographs were sold in card format for the edification and instruction of an audience conditioned to find "Abdul Kerim Fade" equivalent to a zoologic specimen.

"A TOLERABLY COMFORTABLE PARLOUR"

By the time of Greene's 1855 excavations at Medinet-Habu, the Nile voyage was no longer a solitary exploration. With regular steamship service between Egypt and Europe in place since 1835, the British consul complained that he was overwhelmed by the number of Nile voyagers, at least fifty in 1843 alone! As more and more people came to Egypt, popular mooring places along the Nile took on a festive air, as David Roberts indicated in this lithograph of Philae (fig. 7). On 3 February 1854, the English artist Edward Lear wrote to his sister from the Island of Philae where he had spent the last eight days sketching. He and his party had "swept out rooms in the great temple and have been quite comfortable in them during our stay. Three or four English boats have generally been on the island, so we have had dinner parties and music every evening nearly."[42]

Lear's choice of quarters was not unusual: when not on their boats, travelers camped in temples and tombs. The American Sarah Haight described her night's accommodations:

> Our place of rest for the night was a large tomb, excavated in the solid rock, in the side of the hill, with one end opening on a sort of terrace. Being well swept out, and spread with carpets and mattresses around the sides, it formed a tolerably comfortable parlour with divans and etc. In the center a table was arranged, by placing several canteen boxes side by side, which, with a clean white table-cloth and sundry articles of dinnerware wore quite a promising aspect. . . . My sleeping apartment, separated by a curtain from the dining room in front, was the nook where had been the sarcophagus of some Pharaoh or other.[43]

The original inhabitants evicted by nineteenth-century guests frequently fueled the latter's cooking fires. Mrs. Haight described the merry crackling of a fire fueled by bitumen-laden mummy bits.

By the mid 1850's, the itinerary for a Nile voyage had become standardized. Busch's *Guide for Travellers in Egypt* (1857) described the "common tour":

> It begins with Alexandria, which together with its curiosities, may be seen in three or four days, thence by train to Cairo where at least a week may be spent in seeing everything. . . . From Cairo, the journey to upper Egypt is generally continued by water, visiting Thebes, and up the stream to Assuan and the island of Philae, which ends the tour. This tour requires—unless the wind on the Nile be very favourable, and flying visits only be made to the different towns and antiquities of the country—at least twelve weeks.[44]

Railway travel between Alexandria and Cairo began in 1855, but beyond Cairo travelers still moved to the ancient rhythms of the river, waiting for the favorable winds and high waters of winter. Anyone venturing beyond Cairo required the services of a *Dragoman,* the general factotum of all Egyptian journeys, who contracted for the boat, bought the provisions, arranged for horses or donkeys when needed, and acted as interpreter and guide. Contemporary guidebooks offered sample contracts and advised the traveler to sign them at a European Consulate. Travelers could rent a large *dahabieh* or a smaller *canga* for the Nile voyage, depending on the size of the party, their taste for luxury, and their resources. (The large *dahabieh* chartered by Francis Frith for his 1856 excursion can be seen in his photograph of the landing at Philae [p. 80].) In either case, they left the age of steam behind as they proceeded south up river under sail when the winds were favorable, resorting to oars and tow ropes when the wind shifted direction.

Every travel guide warned, as Busch did, "In choosing a bark it is particularly necessary to ascertain that it has been recently sunk, which is done to destroy the vermin, especially rats and bugs."[45] The English artist W.H. Bartlett gave his readers a cautionary tale of a first night on the Nile when this procedure had not been followed.

The boat, when fitted up, was quite a snug little ark, a world in itself. I went on board, proud of my floating home. I was monarch of all I surveyed, and amused myself with arranging every thing in the nicest order; and what with books, pistols, matting carpets, and green blinds, it looked so pretty and so cheerful, and when I lay down on my bed, the breezes were so delightful that I heartily rejoiced. [Later that night, Bartlett's idyll was disturbed.] The scoundrel of a Reis [the title given the head of

Figure 7

David Roberts
The Hypaethral Temple at Philae, called the Pharaoh's Bed, 1838–1839
Color lithograph, 19 x 12-1/2 in.
Private collection

the crew] had neglected to sink the boat as he had promised, and from every chink and crevice in the old planks hundreds came forth scenting the blood of an Englishman; books, matting, and clothing were all in a swarm with the disgusting vermin. . . .[46]

The first night on the Nile was not so fraught with difficulty for everyone. Gustave Flaubert's journal attests to the sense of freedom as the voyage finally began:

First night on the Nile. State of contentment and of lyricism: I gesticulate, recite lines from Bouilhet, cannot bring myself to go to bed: I think of Cleopatra. The water is yellow and very smooth; a few stars. Well-wrapped in my cloak I fall asleep on my camp bed on deck. Such rapture.[47]

Five years before her efforts on behalf of the wounded in the Crimean War, Florence Nightingale was packed off to Egypt with family friends after refusing what her disgusted parents were reasonably sure would be her last proposal of marriage. Traveling in the fall of 1849, as were Flaubert and Du Camp, her description of the first night on the Nile illustrates the different associations travelers brought to Egypt.[48] In general, Egypt's allure for the French lay in its romantic and exotic quality, while the British traveler, at a time when the evangelical movement in England was increasingly strong, sought Biblical associations there. Miss Nightingale's Egypt was the site where Moses had been found in the bulrushes, not an occasion for fevered dreams of Cleopatra, as her December 4 letter home makes clear:

[The party rode donkeys to their mooring place] . . . Had a beautiful sunset ride through the alleys of bulrushes, out of which you can see nothing but the sky, down to Ibrahim Pacha's new palace, by the riverside, where Mr. L. had moored our boat. The pyramids loomed large in the twilight—the frogs sang—and the deep quiet of those solemn waters was so soothing. I gathered a nosegay of roses on the Island of Roda (Moses' island) to take with us—the last rose of Egypt. Now we are floating up so gently, so smoothly, that you can hardly perceive the motion.[49]

EGYPT ON GLASS

In September 1856, Francis Frith, accompanied by his friend Francis Wenham, left England for Egypt on the first of three photographic expeditions to the Middle East.[50] Frith's arrival in Egypt, armed with the new wet collodion on glass negative process, signaled the end of the era of the gentleman amateur and the beginning of commercial photography in Egypt. In 1854, after cornering the market in Greek raisins, the thirty-two-year-old Frith took his profits and retired to a life of leisure.[51] He devoted this new-found leisure to photography, an interest of his since at least 1853, when he and a couple of friends started the Liverpool Photographic Society. As Frith the gentleman amateur experimented with the wet collodion on glass negative process recently introduced by Frederick Scott Archer, Frith the entrepreneur was struck by the commercial possibilities for photographs printed from the glass plates. He realized that with proper care the glass plate negative could yield thousands of sharply detailed photographic prints and would revolutionize the printing and sale of photographs. He predicted that large, reasonably priced editions of photographs for a growing middle-class market would replace the expensive, deluxe editions of salted paper prints collected by a small group of antiquarian connoisseurs.

A photographic expedition to Egypt and the Holy Land offered Frith the possibility of turning his idea to profit while enjoying an adventure. Popular interest in Egypt, fueled by a steady stream of travel accounts, pictures, artifacts, and elaborate recreations at the Universal Expositions of 1851, 1855, and 1867, had grown rather than diminished (pp. 145, 146). Because the ultimate investigation of Egypt, the Egyptian tour, remained a privilege of wealth, the Victorian middle class was ripe for a surrogate Egyptian tour. The enthusiastic response to six volumes of color lithographs by British artist David Roberts, *Views in the Holy Land, Syria, Idumai, Arabia, Egypt and Nubia* (1842–1849), may have encouraged Frith's plan.[52] Roberts' work was popular and profitable because it supplied something earlier, scholarly records of archaeological sites had lacked: a sense of the color and incident a traveler might see in Egypt (figs. 7, 8). The lesson was not lost on Frith. Parties of Victorian tourists (pp. 87, 90), exotically costumed natives (p. 88), and a crocodile, immobilized by the taxidermist's skill (pp. 75, 147), inhabit Frith's carefully staged photographs.

Figure 8

David Roberts
***Fragment of the Colossus of Memnon at Thebes*, 1838–1839**
Color lithograph, 19 x 12-1/2 in.
Private collection

Frith wrote a short description which appeared opposite every photograph in the published volumes. He singled out interesting features which might have been missed in the profusion of details recorded by the large-format photographs. At the Ramesseum at Qurna, Thebes (p. 87): "On the right shoulder of the colossus is the prenomen of Ramses II. On the head may be seen the barbarous inscriptions of modern travellers—instance of a mania as reprehensible as it is childish." As he escorted them through the necropolis surrounding the Pyramids at Saqqara, he cautioned his readers to watch out for mummy-pits into which an unwary stroller could tumble (p. 94). The combination of Frith's voice and the camera's meticulous transcription of detail made readers feel they were entering the photographed sites beside a knowledgeable and urbane guide.

Francis Frith was a devout Christian as well as an astute businessman, and he had deeper aspirations for his enterprise. He realized that the unquestioned veracity of the photograph could bear compelling witness to the historical truth of the Bible. The photograph of Jerusalem seen from the Mount of Olives did not show an impressive city, but he reminded his audience that, like a "much loved face, such a truthful record is of much more value than the most elaborately beautiful picture" (p. 96). He followed the lead of religious painters, like the Pre-Raphaelite William Holman Hunt who had visited Egypt in 1854, in looking to the East for eye-witness knowledge that would confirm the Scriptures. Attention to Egypt's biblical connections remained important: the site of the first excavation supported by the Egyptian Exploration Fund in 1885 was chosen for its biblical associations.

If the earlier calotypists had grappled with difficulties in transporting equipment and making photographs under Egyptian conditions, Frith's first expedition must have been a logistical nightmare. He carried three cameras, a small stereo camera, a standard 8" x 10" format camera, and a mammoth plate camera which took 16" x 20" plates. Frith's solution for dealing with the cumbersome size of the mammoth plate camera and the demands of the wet plate process was ingenious: " . . . For the purpose of making large pictures (20 inches by 16), I had constructed in London, a wicker-work carriage on wheels, which was, in fact, both camera and developing room, and occasionally sleeping room. . . ."[53] Although the lightweight, wheeled enclosure may have made the mammoth plate camera a bit more maneuverable, it was undoubtedly a chore to deploy it at every stop along the Nile. (Its tracks lead from Frith's boat at Philae [p. 80] and mark the search for a good vantage point at Saqqara [p. 94].)

The decision to use Archer's process and three different size cameras required cases of glass plates, cargo which was as heavy as it was fragile. The wet collodion process was demanding: to make a negative the photographer evenly coated a glass plate with viscous collodion and sensitized it in a bath of silver salts in the darkroom, placed the plate in a negative holder, transported it immediately to the camera for exposure, made the exposure, and hurried back to the darkroom to develop it before the solution dried. What was demanding in a studio was a nightmare in the desert or on the banks of the Nile. Frith had to plan his shot, then set up and adjust the camera or cameras. (He frequently photographed the same view in all three formats.) A darkroom was established a few steps from the camera and stocked with glass plates, jugs of solutions, and distilled water. Then the photographer waited, trying to anticipate the moment when the light would be perfect, to begin the complex choreography of preparing, exposing, and developing the plates. If that were not difficult enough, Frith had to contend with equatorial temperatures:

> The difficulties which I had to overcome in working collodion, in those hot dry climates, were also very serious. When (at the Second Cataract, one thousand miles from the mouth of the Nile, with the thermometer at 110 degrees in my tent) the collodion actually boiled when poured upon the glass plate, I almost despaired of success.[54]

Frith need not have despaired. His work, especially the mammoth plate photographs, was a tremendous success. The size of the photographs and the absolute clarity of detail were perfect for armchair travelers, who could literally lose themselves in the scene. They were the perfect response to the criterion for works of art set by social critic and art historian John Ruskin: "The primal object is to place the spectator, as far as art can do, in the scene represented, and to give him the perfect sensation of its reality, wholly unmodified by the artist's execution."[55] Tastes had changed, empirical description had supplanted romantic reverie:

> There was no practical advantage in being able to count each mortar course in the brick wall of a distant building, but it was nevertheless a pleasure to look at a picture that allowed one to do this. It produced the satisfactory illusion that all was revealed, nothing withheld.[56]

MARKETING EGYPT

Although a small number of serious amateurs continued to make photographs in Egypt, by 1860 commercial practitioners dominated Egyptian photography. On the surface little seemed to have changed as, like the early amateurs, commercial photographers visited Egypt, recorded a Nile journey, and returned home with their photographs. But the photographic representations of Egypt did change. Photographs of mysterious fragments (pp. 58, 65) were replaced by comprehensive views, ordered and simplified by the photographer's vantage point (p. 108). Commercial photographers made photographs that created an ideal, imaginary journey which viewers could experience in their comfortable Victorian parlors as they pored over the plates in a book or clustered around the stereopticon.

In most cases, Egyptian work comprised a discrete portion of photographers' business operations. Frith's Egyptian views constituted no more than 15% of the inventory of over two thousand negatives held by his photographic printing and publishing firm at Reigate (pp. 74–96). Many of the views Frith offered were made by hired photographers such as Frank Mason Good (pp. 115–118), who worked for Frith initially and made at least two trips to the Middle East. Francis Bedford was already a well-known photographer when Queen Victoria commissioned him to accompany the 1862 tour of Egypt undertaken by the Prince of Wales (pp. 105–109).

Brilliantly printed and crisply detailed photographs from glass plate negatives ushered in a golden age of commercial view photography. The practice of view photography was defined by a clear set of expectations shared by photographer and buyer. Views did not suggest or allude to a locale, they delineated it precisely. Dramatic effects of light and shade that might confuse the presentation of a complete, spatially coherent site were avoided. A well-executed photographic view was as much a map as it was a picture.

From these common assumptions photographers had developed a set of strategies which they applied in Egypt. Large-format cameras and lenses stopped down to the smallest aperture yielded an extended depth of field which registered foreground elements and distant objects in sharp focus. Camera angles that emphasized the access into a space and the relationships among structures were preferred. Confronted with the ruined architectural ensembles of Egypt, the photographer might choose an elevated perspective that exposed sequential layers of architectural elements, or position his camera at eye level to reveal an avenue into the ruin. Francis Bedford's photographs, lucid, unemotional descriptions of place, are fine examples of the view aesthetic. He photographed the ruins at Philae, a maze of low crumbling walls and fallen masonry, from an elevated vantage point that spread the jumbled structures before his audience (p. 106). At Luxor where visitors strolled on cleared, level ground, Bedford positioned his camera at eye level (p. 105). Here, the viewer reads the space through his implied ability to walk around the colossal sculptures, inspect the pylon reliefs, and eventually pass through the pylon to the mosque revealed behind it.

Francis Frith was a master at presenting complex spaces. At the Mosque of Sultan Quait-Bey, he used light to diagram the interlocking courtyard spaces (p. 93). Elongated shadows expose gaps in the crumbling walls and point out the entrance to the mosque. The multiple layers of the structure are articulated by sharply lit walls. The lighting emphasizes the coarse layers of masonry and geometric patterns and adds a tactile dimension to the visual experience of exploring the mosque.

The changing pattern of visitors to Egypt created a new market for commercial photographers. Over the course of the nineteenth century, the personal journey of discovery gave way to the fashionable activity of tourism.[57] The scientific photographic documents collected by Du Camp and Greene were replaced by travel albums, assembled from mementos and purchased photographs. The *Tour du Monde,* as these elaborate, personally composed travel albums were called, became a token of membership in an amiable circle of world travelers who lightly sampled the attractions of a place and then moved on. Commercial studios sprang up to provide souvenir photographs and their numbers in Egypt grew as the demand for photographs grew.[58]

Some of these resident photographers, including the French partners Béchard and Délié (pp. 127–129), and the Italian Antonio Beato (pp. 102–104), were Europeans. Others came from parts of the Ottoman Empire, as did the Bonfils family (pp. 113, 114), Pascal Sebah (pp. 130–134, 138), and the three brothers who signed their photographs Abdullah Frères (pp. 139, 140). Yet others belonged to a class of peripatetic photographers who, like photo-journalists today, could be found wherever something new and different presented itself to the camera lens. Felix Beato and his brother-in-law and partner James Robertson, who paused in Egypt on their way to photograph the aftermath of the Indian Mutiny, belong to this last category (pp. 71, 73).

The photographs by Antonio Beato in this exhibition are taken from the Terry Album, one of the most complete examples of the travel album genre (pp. 102–104). Lt. Astley F. Terry of the 60th Royal Rifles compiled four volumes of photographs and memorabilia from India, Ceylon, Burma, Egypt, Malta, England, and Canada, an eloquent testament to the extent of the British Empire. Lt. Terry began his album in 1860 when he was posted to the Nilgiris Hills in Southern India. In the first volume, regimental and commercial photographs, receipts, programs from amateur theatricals, clippings from local newspapers, and invitations to social events record his assignments in India, Burma, and Ceylon. The volume ends with his Egyptian stopover on the return journey to England four years later.

Lt. Terry's brief stay in Egypt was typical of British travelers moving between India and England. Leaving Ceylon shortly after 1 April 1864, he traveled by steamship up the coast of India around the Arabian Peninsula and up the Red Sea. Until the Canal was completed in 1869, passengers disembarked at Suez and continued on to Cairo and Alexandria by rail. On 15 April, Lt. Terry was in Alexandria arranging for first-class passage to England with the Peninsular and Oriental Steam Navigation Co. The brief break in his journey permitted him to visit the major sights around Cairo and Alexandria. The photographs of the Pyramids, Cleopatra's Needle, and Pompey's Pillar, and views of Cairo and Alexandria which he purchased from Beato and Hammerschmidt for inclusion in his album seem to constitute the whole of his Egyptian experience.

ARCHAEOLOGICAL AMUSEMENTS

The ancient ruins that had mesmerized the first amateur photographers remained a mainstay of commercial view photographers. Archaeology, once the esoteric passion of a small set of wealthy dilettantes, became a popular diversion at mid-century as ancient civilizations emerged from the dirt. In 1853, the Assyrian artifacts excavated by Austen Layard joined the Egyptian antiquities on display in the British Museum. Ancient Sumeria was revealed by the Frenchman Paul-Émile Botta, and layers of Biblical history were slowly peeled back in Palestine. The *Illustrated London News* began a regular column devoted to archaeological discoveries in 1856, the same year that Oliver Wendell Holmes addressed the London Academy on the moral implications of archaeological exploration:

> I believe in the spade. It has fed the tribes of mankind. It has furnished them water, coal, iron and gold. And now it is giving them truth—historic truth—the mines of which have never been opened till our time.[59]

Archaeology found its greatest popularizer when the Victorian novelist and journalist Amelia Edwards visited Egypt in 1873–74 on a whim "induced by the weather." She recounted her travels in *A Thousand Miles up the Nile* (1877), which sold briskly and remains one of the most interesting and charming accounts of travel in Egypt. At one moment she could evoke the atmosphere in the great temple at Dendara:

> Without, all was sunshine and splendour; within all was silence and mystery. A heavy death-like smell, as of long imprisoned gases, met us on the threshold. By the half-light that strayed in through the portico, we could see vague outlines of a forest of giant columns. . . .[60]

In the next moment, she is revealing the enormity of archaeological time at Saqqara:

> If Egyptologists are right in ascribing the royal title hieroglyphed on the inner door of this pyramid to Ouenephes, the fourth king of the First Dynasty, then it is the most ancient building in the world. It had been standing from five to seven hundred years when King Cheops began his Great Pyramid at Geezah. It was over two thousand years old when Abraham was born. It is now about six thousand eight hundred years old according to Mariette. . . . One's imagination recoils upon the brink of such a gulf of time.[61]

She lectured on Egypt throughout England and America. At every stop on her popular lecture tours, local shops sold out their stock of stereo views of Egypt. Orders for large cabinet card photographs of Egypt which were advertised on flyers posted at the entrances to the lecture halls quickly followed. Not only was Amelia Edwards good for the photography business, she was good for Egyptian archaeology. As one of the founders of the Egyptian Exploration Fund, she solicited contributions from her enthralled audiences. With her own modest resources, Miss Edwards endowed the first English chair in Egyptology, which was held for forty years by the dean of British Egyptology, Sir Flinders Petrie.

PACKAGING EGYPT

Travel in Egypt changed forever when thirty British citizens under the guidance of Thomas Cook attended the opening of the Suez Canal in November 1869. The modest group faded into insignificance beside the glittering entourages of Emperor Franz Joseph of Austria, Empress Eugénie of France, the Prince and Princess of Wales, and the scores of foreign dignitaries.[62] But ultimately, their presence would overshadow the royal excursions because Thomas Cook's first tour signaled the beginning of the era of mass tourism in Egypt.

In 1841, as the general overseer of the South Midlands Temperance Association, Thomas Cook organized a day trip for the membership on the recently completed Midlands Railroad. The ten-mile trip to Paget's Park in Loughborough, where the excursionists enjoyed games and temperance lectures, grew out of Cook's idea that it would be "a glorious thing . . . if the newly developed powers of the railways and locomotives could be made sub-servient to the cause of Temperance."[63] Thus the package tour was conceived in the union of Victorian self-improve-ment and mechanical ingenuity. In succeeding years Cook's Tours conveyed 165,000 people to the Crystal Palace Exhibition (1851), organized tours to the Universal Exposition in Paris (1855), and made holiday arrangements for destinations throughout Great Britain and the Continent. Thomas Cook and his sons pioneered the use of pre-paid coupons for accommodations, developed travelers' checks, and demanded strict standards in services and lodgings for their clients, which they enforced by frequent inspections.

Cook's Midlands egalitarianism rejected the notion that travel was the privilege of the upper class. If the *hoi-poloi* found travel intellectually improving, so would his unabashedly middle-class clients. The *Cooksii,* as the Egyptians called his groups, drew the scorn of aristocrats. William Russell, the *London Times* war correspondent trav-eling with the Prince and Princess of Wales' party, filed the following disparaging report:

> That it is a nuisance to the ordinary traveller to have his peace broken, to have a flood of people
> poured into a quiet town, to have hotels and steamers crammed, . . . to behold his favourite valley
> filled up with a flood of "mere English, whom no one knows," I am not prepared to deny; but what
> are we to say to "the greatest good of the greatest number?" The people at Alexandria were, as far as I
> could judge, very respectable—it was only in the concrete they became disagreeable. Mr. Brown and
> Miss Clara de Mowbray may be capital companions as individuals, in the abstract, but as "Cook's
> Tourists" they became an aggregate of terrors.[64]

Cook's Tours altered the face of tourism in Egypt as, with the very first tour, single, unattached women joined their groups. The few women who had toured Egypt earlier in the century had done so in the company of a male relative. A testimonial letter to Mr. Cook from "Mathilda," one of the peripatetic new women, makes it quite clear that earlier mores had been superseded. She refuted conventional wisdom that declared her and her sisters

> too independent and adventurous to leave the shores of Old England and thus to plunge into for-
> eign countries not beneath Victoria's sway, with no protecting relatives of any kind. We could ven-
> ture anywhere with such a guide and guardian as Mr. Cook.[65]

Their guide and guardian started from the basic premise that his excursionists needed to be insulated from the reality of Egyptian life. Cook's Tours, with the promise of hundreds of guests, exacted compliance with British norms in transport and accommodation which ultimately blunted the vagaries of travel for everyone. The newly refurbished Shepheard's Hotel and the comfortable cabins of Cook's Steamers replaced the swept-out tomb as lodging.

By 1872, Thomas Cook had taken a total of 400 tourists up the Nile, and in the 1873 season alone, 200 traveled with him. The Cooks were firmly entrenched by the mid-1870's, operating the Nile steamship service under a franchise from the Khedive, the Turkish Viceroy of Egypt, who also appointed them sole agent for the mail. Although other tour operators emerged, like Gaze and Son in the 1870's, Dean and Dawson (1878), John Frame's Tours for Teetotallers (1881), and Hogg's Polytechnic Tours (1886), Cook's Tours was synonymous with the Nile excursion. Their clientele changed yet again when John Cook took over the Egyptian operation and repackaged Egypt as a luxury destination. He built lavish new steamers to replace the Khedive's old fleet and soon even independent travelers sailed on Cook's Steamship Service. By 1880 Murray's Handbook could assure its readers that "for lovers of all that is luxurious in travel, of all that is glorious in memory, of the grand, the beautiful, the picturesque and the strange, Egyptian travel is the perfection of life."[66]

Traffic through the Suez Canal, ease of travel, and long familiarity, all combined to bring more and more people to Egypt. Amelia Edwards described the motley assortment she found in 1874 in the great dining room at Shepheard's Hotel in Cairo:

> Here assemble daily some two to three hundred persons of all ranks, nationalities and pursuits; half of whom are Anglo-Indians homeward or outward bound, European residents, or visitors established in Cairo for the winter. The other half, it may be taken for granted, are going up the Nile. . . . Here are invalids in search of health; artists in search of subjects; sportsmen keen upon crocodile; statesmen out for a holiday; special correspondents alert for gossip; collectors on the scent of papyri and mummies; men of science with only scientific ends in view; and the usual surplus of idlers who travel for the mere love of travel or the satisfaction of purposeless curiosity.[67]

Miss Edwards' catalogue of travelers came to Egypt to savor the sense of overwhelming antiquity and to enjoy its exotic present, but access to these experiences was regulated by the very practice of tourism. The experience of the exotic and the ancient would be mediated by photographic representation.

THE PHARAOH'S FACE

The days when a traveler could forage at Thebes for fragments of mummies and papyri, or chisel off a section of carved relief, were mercifully over. In 1856 Ismail-Pasha had been persuaded to take action to halt the loss of Egyptian artifacts. He appointed the French Egyptologist Auguste Mariette to form an Antiquities Service and establish a museum in Cairo. Casual collectors turned to photographic representations, although a brisk trade in stolen or faked artifacts flourished. Tourists indulged their taste for archaeological collecting with Délié and Béchard's photographs of meticulously arranged objects in the Antiquities Museum (pp. 127–129). The Abdullah Frères' photograph of Mariette's excavation of the temple beneath the Sphinx afforded the vicarious thrill of an archaeological dig (p. 140). More important tourists could be provided with the actual experience, as the Prince of Wales was when a mummy was "discovered" during his 1862 stop at Thebes.

Plundered for their jewelry or the papyri in their wrappings, broken up to make elixirs, and collected as objects of morbid curiosity, mummies had attracted travelers for centuries. The inspiration for pulp novels as well as poetic meditations, the mummy's appeal for the modern traveler was conflicted. While Flaubert exalted the mummy of Cleopatra above any living woman, his traveling companion Maxime Du Camp plundered the necropolis at Thebes:

> I broke up some of the mummies, seeking scarabs in their bitumen-filled bellies; from one I took its gilded feet, from another its head with its long tresses of hair, from a third its dry black hands.[68]

Mariette's intervention rescued a few of the ancient dead and moved them to a new resting place in the Cairo Museum. They were joined in 1881 by some of the most illustrious rulers of Egypt. Earlier that year, the photographer/archaeologist Émile Brugsch had noticed unusual artifacts appearing on the black market. He tracked their source to a community of grave robbers, who were coerced into revealing a great cache of royal mummies hidden near Dar el-Bahri. The gilded mummy cases of Ramses II, his father Seti I, Queen Nefertari, Amenhotep I, and Thotmes II were raised from their hiding place and carried back down the Nile. Five years later Egyptologists began to unwrap them for study. (The photograph on p. 142 appears to have been made as the mummies were being unwrapped. If so, Brugsch was probably the photographer.) In May 1886 the mummy of Ramses II was unwrapped in the presence of the Khedive of Egypt.[69] The desiccated face of the great ruler whose likeness was carved on the cliffs at Abu Simbel was revealed (p. 141). Stripped of mystery, the profile mug shot reveals a face which Gaston Maspero described having a "somewhat unintelligent expression, slightly brutish perhaps, but haughty and firm of purpose."[70] The mummy of Ramses II, 19th Dynasty Pharaoh of Upper and Lower Egypt, had survived for over three thousand years to become a late nineteenth-century scientific exhibit and curiosity.

A SEMBLANCE OF EGYPT

Although earlier travelers had been insulated to some degree from Egyptian life by their resources and status as Europeans, in the last quarter of the nineteenth century, visitors floated through Egypt in a veritable envelope of Western comfort. As the distance between tourists and the realities of Egyptian life grew, photographic representations came to provide a simulacrum of the experiences they avoided. Staged commercial photographs recapitulated exotic street scenes which tourists were convinced were enacted daily in the narrow streets their guides hurried them past. Costumed natives posed as dung sellers (p. 119), date cake sellers (p. 113), sweet sellers (p. 132), orange sellers

(p. 124), water carriers (p. 133), and yarn spinners (p. 130). The same person could appear in many scenes, variously identified as a rag picker, a rabbi, or a knife sharpener.[71]

Orientalist genre paintings conditioned the expectations from which the photographs derived. Paintings with almost photographic detail depicting colorful and exotic incidents had been extremely popular since the early part of the century. Commercial photographs and Orientalist paintings came to reinforce each other, as painters worked from photographs and photographers emulated paintings. The *Rug Merchant* by Jean-Léon Gérôme (fig. 9) and *The Rug Dealer* by Félix Bonfils (p. 114) are equivalent images called into existence by a market for fabricated incidents from an alien culture.

Commercial photographers offered a category of photographs called types, portraits of ethnically costumed individuals (pp. 121, 125, 131, 135–137). Although very few of the photographs portrayed named individuals, several commercial operators photographed Sheik Sadad (p. 123). Identified as a descendent of the Prophet, the Sheik was

Figure 9

Jean-Léon Gérôme
Le Marchant de tapis au Caire
(The Rug Merchant at Cairo), 1887
Oil on canvas, 83.5 x 64.7 cm.
The Minneapolis Institute of Arts,
Minneapolis, Minn.

seen as the quintessential Islamic *type* rather than as a unique individual. And, indeed, the Sheik's portrait was offered to customers as part of the photographer's stock of ethnographic images.

Presented in vaguely ethnographic terms, studies of anonymous costumed types ran the gamut from banal studio set-ups (p. 125) through exploitative stereotypes (p. 137). Primarily studies of women, they frequently had subtle erotic overtones, as in Béchard's carefully posed study of a veiled woman waiting passively on a secluded balcony (p. 121). Western viewers, conditioned by the myth of harems stocked with languorously compliant women, could easily read the message. The heavy-lidded reverie of an unveiled woman was a bit more explicit, the smoldering cigarette evoking sensual states associated with the use of hashish (p. 137). Occasionally, through some alchemy of photographer and subject, an emotionally resonant portrait was produced (p. 136). The photograph of a black woman, identified only as the type of a negress, transcends the genre.

EPILOGUE

Since the invention of photography, a symbiotic relationship has grown up between it and the activity of travel. Document and impetus, photographic representation became inseparable from actual journey. In the decades following 1839 when the first camera was set up in Egypt, travel photography evolved from a vehicle for personal or scientific exploration to a business catering to armchair travelers and tourists. J. B. Greene's photographs were scientific field notes. Félix Teynard recorded his "sensations." Francis Frith packaged a simulated Nile voyage for the entertainment and edification of Victorian households. Henri Béchard supplied a cast of types posed in exotic scenes for the consumption of the idly curious. The changes in photographic practice marked the changing character of travel in Egypt. The traveler's exploration of the world gave way to the tourist's avid consumption of sights. Throughout it all, Egypt continued to exert its unmistakable allure.

It may be said of some very old places, as of some very old books, that they are destined to be forever new. The nearer we approach them, the more remote they seem; the more we study them, the more we have yet to learn. Time augments rather than diminishes their everlasting novelty; and to our descendants of a thousand years hence it may safely be predicted that they will be even more fascinating than to ourselves. This is true of many ancient lands, but of no place is it so true as of Egypt. . . . interest never flags—the subject never palls upon us—the mine is never exhausted.[72]

Over 100 years later, Amelia Edwards' prediction holds true. The photographs made there in the nineteenth century have only amplified Egypt's powerful hold on the Western imagination. Our late twentieth-century dreams of Nile voyages to ancient ruins are woven from the images born in the marriage of light and chemistry in the nineteenth century.

NOTES

1. J. Christopher Herold, *Bonaparte in Egypt* (New York: Harper & Row, 1962), 155.

2. Mark Twain, *Innocents Abroad* (New York: MacMillan Co., 1927), 509.

3. Baron Jean-Baptiste Fourier, "Préface Historique" in vol. 1 of *Description de l'Égypte* (Paris: l'Imprimerie impériale, 1809), i.

4. Diodorus Siculus, *Library of History,* vol. 2, trans. C.H. Oldfather (New York: 1933), 239.

5. Quoted in C.C. Gillispie, "Historical Introduction," in vol. 1 of *Monuments of Egypt: The Napoleonic Edition, The Complete Archaeological Plates from La Description de l'Égypte,* ed. Charles Coulson Gillispie and Michel Dewachter (Princeton: Princeton Architectural Press, 1987), 18.

6. The political and imperial implications of European study of the Middle East were presented in an important critical study by Edward Said, *Orientalism* (New York: Random House, 1978). While it is not the intention of this essay to provide a critical interpretation of events in Egypt in the nineteenth century, Said's reading of Western scholarship regarding the East provides a rich counterpoint to a narrative usually given from the European perspective.

7. Fourier, iii.

8. C.C. Gillispie, 1–29, provides a detailed account of the events leading to the establishment of the Commission of Arts and Sciences, its composition and activities, as well as the publication of its work in the *Description de l'Égypte.*

9. Pietro Della Valle, *The Pilgrim: The Journeys of Pietro Della Valle,* trans. and abridged by George Bull (London: The Folio Society, 1989).

10. Stephen Jay Gould and Rosamond Wolff Purcell, in *Finders, Keepers: Eight Collectors* (New York: W. W. Norton and Co., 1992) describe one of the more lavish of the eighteenth-century cabinets, that of Peter the Great of Russia. Purcell's extraordinary photographs and Gould's engaging text disclose the bizarre array of objects brought together in the cabinet of curiosities.

11. Dominique Vivant Denon, *Voyage dans la Basse et la Haute Égypte,* ed. Raoul Brunon (Paris: Gerard Watelet, 1990), 35.

12. The title for this section is taken from Brian Fagan, *The Rape of the Nile: Tomb Robbers, Tourists, and Archaeologists in Egypt* (New York: Charles Scribner, 1975), a complete and highly readable account of the colorful characters and incidents of this period in Egyptian history from which the information about Drovetti, Salt, and Belzoni is taken.

13. Obelisks had been imperial trophies since Roman days when Augustus transported the first one to Rome. The city plan of Rome devised by Pope Sixtus V was organized around the re-erection of obelisks brought to Rome over a thousand years earlier. By the end of the nineteenth century, Rome, Paris, London, and New York boasted obelisks looted from Egypt. Captain Saint-Maur is quoted in Karl E. Meyer, *The Pleasure of Archaeology* (New York: Atheneum, 1971), 62.

14. Giovanni Belzoni's *Narrative of the Operations and Recent Discoveries within the Pyramids, Temples, Tombs, and Excavations, in Egypt* (London: Murray, 1820), is one of the most entertaining accounts of early explorations in Egypt. Howard Carter, the discoverer of Tutankhamen's tomb, attributed his interest in Egyptian archaeology to reading Belzoni.

15. Quoted in Raymond Schwab, *The Oriental Renaissance: Europe's Rediscovery of India and the East 1680–1880,* trans. by Gene Patterson-Black and Victor Reinking (New York: Columbia University Press, 1984), 12.

16. The spectrum of artistic engagement with the Middle East and North Africa was the subject in 1984 of a joint exhibition by the Royal Academy of Arts and the National Gallery of Art. The profusely illustrated catalogue accompanying the exhibition contains informative essays and brief biographical notices of the artists. *The Orientalists: Delacroix to Matisse, European Painters in North Africa and the Near East,* ed. MaryAnne Stevens (London: Royal Academy of Arts, 1984).

17. The Arabic texts which make up the collection of stories known as *One Thousand and One Arabian Nights* were first collected, translated, and published by Antoine Galland in 1717.

18. Quoted in Francis Steegmuller, *Flaubert in Egypt: A Sensibility on Tour* (Chicago: Academy, 1972), 11.

19. Percy Bysshe Shelley, "Alastor; Or, the Spirit of Solitude," in vol. 2 of *The Norton Anthology of English Literature,* 5th ed. (New York: W.W. Norton, 1986), 671.

20. My understanding of this print was greatly enhanced by discussions with Michael Wilson.

21. F. Gladstone Bratton, *A History of Egyptian Archaeology* (London: Robert Hale, 1967), 37–51, narrates the history of the decipherment of hieroglyphics, a fascinating tale of scholarly feuds and brilliant detective work.

22. Quoted in "Report," in *History of Photography,* by Josef Maria Eder, trans. by E. Epstean (New York: Columbia University Press, 1945; reprint ed. 1972) 234–235.

23. See short biographical notice in Nissan Perez, *Focus East: Early Photography in the Near East, 1839–1885* (New York: Abrams, 1988), 169. Frédéric Goupil-Fesquet, *Voyage d'Horace Vernet en Orient* (Bruxelles: 1844), gives a sprightly description of the conditions under which travelers made photographs in 1839.

24. Perez, *Focus East,* 181.

25. Goupil-Fesquet, *Voyage,* 82.

26. Although Taylor's series had been recognized as a seminal influence on nineteenth-century travel books, Eugenia Parry Janis and André Jammes, *The Art of French Calotype* (Princeton: Princeton University Press, 1983), 48–53, first pointed out the key role played by the *Voyages pittoresques* in the development of a calotype aesthetic in France.

27. Larry Schaaf, *Out of the Shadows: Herschel, Talbot, and the Invention of Photography* (New Haven: Yale University Press, 1992), presents the fascinating early history of Talbot's development of a photographic process. Schaaf elucidates the circumstances surrounding Talbot's discovery and the length of time between discovery and announcement.

28. A recent, unpublished dissertation by Nancy Keeler (University of Texas at Austin, 1991), provides a much-needed history of Bayard's parallel discovery.

29. The elaboration of paper negative processes are discussed by Janis and Jammes, *The Art of French Calotype.* Gustave Le Gray's contributions are described in Eugenia Parry Janis, *The Photography of Gustave Le Gray* (Chicago: University of Chicago Press, 1987).

30. The most complete description of Du Camp's project is found in Elizabeth Anne McCauley, "The Photographic Adventure of Maxime Du Camp," in *The Library Chronicle of the University of Texas at Austin* 19 (1982), 19–51.

31. The conjunction of literary inspiration and sensual experience is most apparent in Gustave Flaubert's novel *Salammbo* in which he models the princess of Carthage on an Egyptian prostitute. Said, *Orientalism,* locates the Western search for sensual experience in the East in the West's perception of non-Europeans as a degraded and compliant people.

32. Alexander Kinglake, *Eothen* (London: Murray, 1845), 27.

33. Gustave Flaubert, "Letter to his mother of 15 April 1850," in *Oeuvres completes de Gustave Flaubert* (Paris: Hachette, 1910), 13:32.

34. Maxime Du Camp, *Souvenirs littéraries,* vol.1 (Paris: Hachette, 1882), 424.

35. Du Camp had a complete set of his negatives printed and presented them to the Institute of France on his return. Printed on albumen paper, the 214 prints give a much clearer idea of what interested Du Camp photographically than does the Blanquart-Évrard publication. Bibliothéque de l'Institut, Reserve folio N.S. 754.

36. The publisher's preference for images of ancient Egypt is documented in correspondence between Du Camp and publishers Gide et Baudry in a private collection. Du Camp's interest in Arabic led him to hire a tutor in Cairo to teach him the language and to help him compile an Arabic grammar.

37. Quoted in Julia Ballerini, "Photography Conscripted: Horace Vernet, Gerard de Nerval and Maxime Du Camp in Egypt," unpublished doctoral dissertation, City University of New York, 1987, 223.

38. A copy of Teynard's passport was made available to me by his descendents. A full discussion of Teynard's background and work may be found in Kathleen Howe, *Félix Teynard: Calotypes of Egypt, A Catalogue Raisonné* (New York: Kraus, Hershkowitz, & Weston, 1992).

39. Teynard's description of his journey is taken from the "Introduction" to *Égypte et Nubie,* the text of which is reproduced in Howe, *Félix Teynard,* 109–111.

40. Théodule Dévéria's letter to François-Joseph Chabas is quoted in Bruno Jammes, "J.B. Greene, an American Calotypist," *History of Photography* 5, no. 4, (1981) 305. Dévéria was also interested in photography. He made landscape photographs at Fontainebleau as well as making photographs of monuments and excavation sites in Egypt.

41. Howe, *Félix Teynard,* 72.

42. Quoted in Christopher Pick, *Egypt: A Traveller's Anthology* (London: John Murray, 1991), 197, from Edward Lear, *Selected Letters* (Oxford: Oxford University Press, 1988).

43. Sarah Haight, *Letters from the Old World* (New York: 1840), 87.

44. Moritz Busch, trans. by W. C. Wrankmore, *Guide for Travellers in Egypt and Adjacent Countries Subject to the Pasha* (London: Trubner & Co., 1857), 30.

45. Busch, 74.

46. W.H. Bartlett, *The Nile Boat* (London: 1850), 117.

47. Steegmuller, *Flaubert in Egypt,* 35.

48. The two parties may have crossed paths in Egypt. Flaubert described an English family among the passengers on the steamer from Alexandria to Cairo: "Passengers: . . . an English family, hideous; the mother looks like a sick old parrot (because of the green eyeshade attached to her bonnet) . . ." (Steegmuller, *Flaubert in Egypt,* 35). If so, that encounter would probably have been the only one. The English party went up river in early December while Du Camp and Flaubert lingered in Cairo for three months.

49. Florence Nightingale, *Letters from Egypt: A Journey on the Nile 1849–1850,* selected and introduced by Anthony Sattin (New York: Weidenfeld & Nicolson, 1987), 41–42.

50. Frith's views of Egypt and the Holy Land were published in at least eight separate editions from 1858 to 1862, and individual views may appear in multiple publications. Photographs from his first expedition were published as *Egypt and Palestine Photographed and Described by Frances Frith*, 2 vols. (London: J.S. Virtue, 1858–1860).

51. Douglas Nickel presented the initial research for a proposed dissertation on Frances Frith at the April 6, 1991, Frick Symposium, New York, in an unpublished paper, "Christianity, Positivism, and Photography: The Case of Francis Frith." My discussion of the details of Frith's life and the association of Frith's photographs with his religious beliefs are informed by Nickel's presentation.

52. Perez, *Focus East,* 164.

53. Quoted from Frith's *Egypt and Palestine,* vol. 2 by Julia Van Haaften, *Egypt and the Holy Land in Historic Photographs: 77 Views by Francis Frith* (New York: Dover, 1980), xi.

54. Quoted in Van Haaften, xi.

55. Quoted in Michael Burton, *The Pre-Raphaelite Camera* (Boston: 1985), 102.

56. John Szarkowski, *Photography Until Now* (New York: Museum of Modern Art, 1989), 71.

57. The changing philosophical and intellectual meaning of travel from antiquity to the present is the subject of Eric Leed, *The Mind of the Traveler: From Gilgamesh to Global Tourism* (New York: Basic Books, 1991).

58. For a long time only the names stamped on photographs pasted in old albums were known, until Perez, *Focus East,* restored their identities and located their studios. The information in this section comes from the biographical dictionary in his study.

59. *Proceedings of the London Academy XXV* (1856), 422.

60. Amelia Edwards, *A Thousand Miles up the Nile,* 2nd ed. (New York: A.L. Burt, 1888), 113.

61. Edwards, *A Thousand Miles,* 48.

62. Félix Teynard attended the ceremonies as the invited guest of the Khedive of Egypt. Adolphe Braun, a commercial photographer celebrated for his views of the Alps, also attended and during his visit made a few photographs, such as that of Philae (p. 126).

63. Quoted in Edmund Swinglehurst, *The Romantic Journey: The Story of Thomas Cook and Victorian Travel* (New York: Harper & Row, 1974), 14. Swinglehurst, and Piers Brendon, *Thomas Cook: 150 Years of Popular Tourism* (London: Secker & Warburg, 1991), relate the history of the growth of Cook's Tours and its impact on tourism.

64. Quoted in Brendon, *Thomas Cook,* 126–127.

65. Quoted in Leed, *The Mind of the Traveler,* 288.

66. Murray, *Handbook for Travellers in Egypt* (London: Murray, 1880), 9.

67. Amelia Edwards, *A Thousand Miles,* 3.

68. Du Camp, *Le Nil* (Paris: Librarie Nouvelle, 1855), 340.

69. James Baikie, *A Century of Excavation in the Land of the Pharaohs* (New York: Fleming H. Revell, 1936), 158–163.

70. The French Egyptologist Gaston Maspero became the head of the Egyptian Antiquities Service and the director of the Cairo Museum upon Mariette's death in 1881. He is quoted in Baike, *A Century of Excavation,* 162.

71. Perez, *Focus East,* 107.

72. Amelia Edwards, *Pharaohs, Fellahs and Explorers* (New York: Harper & Brothers, 1892), 3.

SELECTED PLATES

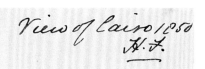

PLATE 1
Anton Schranz
Maltese (1801–?)
View of Cairo, c. 1852
Albumen print

48

PLATE 2
Maxime Du Camp
French (1822–1894)
Colossus of Memnon, 1850
Salt print from paper negative

PLATE 3
Maxime Du Camp
French (1822–1894)
Qurna, Peristyle of the Tomb of Ozymandias, 1850
Salt print from paper negative

PLATE 4
Maxime Du Camp
French (1822–1894)
Great Temple of Isis, Philae, 1850
Salt print from paper negative

PLATE 5
Maxime Du Camp
French (1822–1894)
Temple of Amada, Nubia, 1850
Salt print from paper negative

PLATE 6
Maxime Du Camp
French (1822–1894)
Doumos Palms, Upper Egypt, 1850
Salt print from paper negative

53

PLATE 7
Ernst Benecke
French (dates unknown)
Sheik Mokba and Members of his Tribe, Sinai, 1852
Salt print from paper negative

54

PLATE 8
Félix Teynard
French (1817–1892)
Temple of Karnak at Thebes, 1851-52
Salt print from paper negative

55

PLATE 9
Félix Teynard
French (1817–1892)
Korosko, Sycamores and Encampment, 1851–52
Salt print from paper negative

56

PLATE 10
Félix Teynard
French (1817–1892)
Assiut, Modern Constructions, The Divan, 1851–52
Salt print from paper negative

PLATE 11
Félix Teynard
French (1817–1892)
Monument Carved into the Bedrock
PIllars and Carved Sculptures, left side, Ed-Derr, 1851–52
Salt print from paper negative

PLATE 12
Félix Teynard
French (1817–1892)
Helmsman and Sailor, c. 1851–52
Salt print from paper negative

PLATE 13
Félix Teynard
French (1817–1892)
Hemi-Speos—Colossi of the Exterior Section, Gerf Hussein, 1851–52
Salt print from paper negative

60

PLATE 14
Félix Teynard
French (1817–1892)
Temple of Hathor, Dendara, c. 1851–52
Salt print from paper negative

PLATE 15
Pierre Tremaux
French (1818–?)
Nubian Woman, 1853–54
Salt print from paper negative

PLATE 16
John Beasley Greene
American (1832–1856)
View of the Hypostyle Hall, Karnak, 1854
Salt print from paper negative

PLATE 17
John Beasley Greene
American (1832–1856)
Ramses Me' i'amoun, Medinet-Habu, 1854
Salt print from paper negative

64

PLATE 18
John Beasley Greene
American (1832–1856)
Abu Simbel, Statue of Woman, 1854
Salt print from paper negative

PLATE 19
John Beasley Greene
American (1832–1856)
Second Cataract of the Nile, 1854
Salt print from paper negative

PLATE 20
John Beasley Greene
American (1832–1856)
Colossus of Memnon, 1854
Salt print from paper negative

PLATE 21
Robert Murray
British (dates unknown)
View of Bulak at Cairo, 1856
Salt print from paper negative

PLATE 22
Anonymous
(Probably French)
Cactus Grove, 1850's
Salt print from paper negative

69

PLATE 23
Anonymous
Street in Cairo, 1850's
Salt print from paper negative

70

PLATE 24
James Robertson & Felix Beato
British (1813–after 1881) and Italian (c. 1830–1906?)
Mosque at Cairo, 1857
Albumen print from glass negative

PLATE 25
James Robertson & Felix Beato
British (1813–after 1881) and Italian (c. 1830–1906?)
Pyramids with Pool of Water, 1857
Salt print from glass negative

PLATE 26
James Robertson & Felix Beato
British (1813–after 1881) and Italian (c. 1830–1906?)
Fountain in the Mosque of Mohammed Ali, 1857
Albumen print from glass negative

73

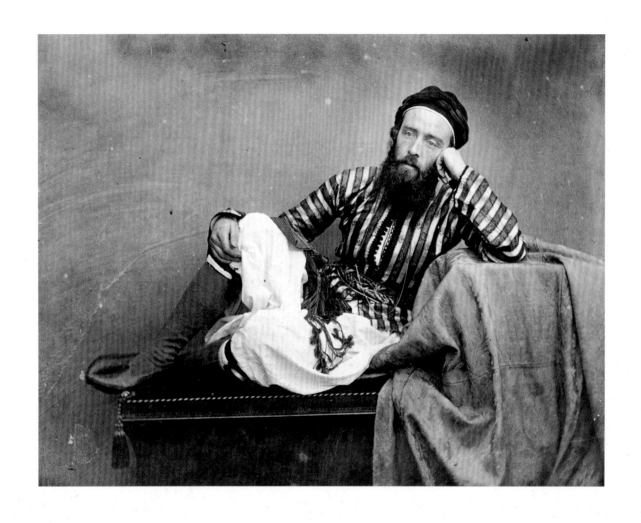

PLATE 27
Francis Frith
British (1822–1898)
Turkish Summer Costume, Self-portrait, c. 1858
Albumen print from glass negative

PLATE 28
Francis Frith
British (1822–1898)
Crocodile on Sand Bank, c. 1858
Albumen print from glass negative

PLATE 29
Francis Frith
British (1822–1898)
Temple at Kom Ombo, 1858
Albumen print from glass negative

76

PLATE 30
Francis Frith
British (1822–1898)
Mount Serbal from the Wâdi Feyran, 1858
Albumen print from glass negative

PLATE 31
Francis Frith
British (1822–1898)
Mount Horeb, 1858
Albumen print from glass negative

PLATE 32
Francis Frith
British (1822–1898)
Mosque of Emir al Aqmar, 1858
Albumen print from glass negative

PLATE 33
Francis Frith
British (1822–1898)
Hypaethral Temple, Philae, 1858
Albumen print from glass negative

PLATE 34
Francis Frith
British (1822–1898)
Temple of Karnak from the Southeast, 1858
Albumen print from glass negative

PLATE 35
Francis Frith
British (1822–1898)
Cairo from the Citadel, First View, 1858
Albumen print from glass negative

PLATE 36
Francis Frith
British (1822–1898)
Cairo from the Citadel, Second View, 1858
Albumen print from glass negative

PLATE 37
Francis Frith
British (1822–1898)
Cairo from the Citadel, Second View (variant), 1858
Albumen print from glass negative

84

PLATE 38
Francis Frith
British (1822–1898)
Pyramids of Dahshur from the Southwest, 1858
Albumen print from glass negative

PLATE 39
Francis Frith
British (1822–1898)
Pyramids of Dahshur from the East, 1858
Albumen print from glass negative

PLATE 40
Francis Frith
British (1822–1898)
Ramesseum at Qurna, Thebes, 1858
Albumen print from glass negative

PLATE 41
Francis Frith
British (1822–1898)
Ramesseum at Qurna, Thebes, second view, 1858
Albumen print from glass negative

PLATE 42
Francis Frith
British (1822–1898)
Street View of Cairo, 1858
Albumen print from glass negative

PLATE 43
Francis Frith
British (1822–1898)
Statues on the Plain of Thebes, 1858
Albumen print from glass negative

90

PLATE 44
Francis Frith
British (1822–1898)
Mosque of Sultan Quait-Bey, 1858
Albumen print from glass negative

PLATE 45
Francis Frith
British (1822–1898)
The Second Pyramid from the Southeast, 1858
Albumen print from glass negative

PLATE 46
Francis Frith
British (1822–1898)
The Great Pyramid and the Great Sphinx, 1858
Albumen print from glass negative

PLATE 47
Francis Frith
British (1822–1898)
The Pyramids of Saqqara from the Northeast, 1858
Albumen print from glass negative

94

PLATE 48
Francis Frith
British (1822–1898)
Cheops' Pyramid at Giza from the Southwest, 1858
Albumen print from glass negative

PLATE 49
Francis Frith
British (1822–1898)
Jerusalem from the Mount of Olives, 1858
Albumen print from glass negative

PLATE 50
Louis de Clercq
French (1836–1901)
Assiut, Palace of the Viceroy, c. 1859
Albumen print from paper negative

PLATE 51
Louis de Clercq
French (1836–1901)
Edfu, Interior Colonnade, c. 1859
Albumen print from paper negative

PLATE 52
Henry Cammas
French (1813–?)
Pyramid and Sphinx, c. 1860
Salt print from paper negative

PLATE 53
Gustave Le Gray
French (1820–1882)
Dendara, Temple of Hathor, c. 1870
Albumen print from paper negative

PLATE 54
W. Hammerschmidt
German (dates unknown)
Gate of the Barrage, 1860's
Albumen print from glass negative

101

PLATE 55
Antonio Beato
Italian (c. 1825–1903)
View from the Citadel, Greater Cairo, c. 1864
from the Astley F. Terry album
Albumen print from glass negative

102

PLATE 56
Antonio Beato
Italian (c. 1825–1903)
The Sphinx and the Great Pyramid, c. 1864
from the Astley F. Terry album
Albumen print from glass negative

PLATE 57
Antonio Beato
Italian (c. 1825–1903)
The Pyramids, c. 1864
from the Astley F. Terry album
Albumen print from glass negative

104

PLATE 58
Francis Bedford
British (1816–1894)
View at Luxor, 1862
Albumen print from glass negative

PLATE 59
Francis Bedford
British (1816–1894)
View of Philae, 1862
Albumen print from glass negative

PLATE 60
Francis Bedford
British (1816–1894)
Thebes, General View of Karnak, 1862
Albumen print from glass negative

PLATE 61
Francis Bedford
British (1816–1894)
View at Dendara, 1862
Albumen print from glass negative

PLATE 62
Francis Bedford
British (1816–1894)
Temple at Medinet-Habu, Thebes, 1862
Albumen print from glass negative

109

PLATE 63
Sergeant James McDonald
British (dates unknown)
View from the Summit of Mount Serbal, Looking Northeast, 1868
Albumen print from glass negative

PLATE 64
Sergeant James McDonald
British (dates unknown)
Non-commissioned Officers of the Royal Engineers, Sinai Survey, c. 1868
Albumen print from glass negative

PLATE 65
Sergeant James McDonald
British (dates unknown)
Wâdi Nakhleh with Distant View of Mount Serbal, 1868
Albumen print from glass negative

PLATE 66
Félix Bonfils
French (1831–1885)
Date Cake Sellers, Cairo, 1870's
Albumen print from glass negative

113

PLATE 67
Félix Bonfils
French (1831–1885)
Rug Dealer, Cairo, 1870's
Albumen print from glass negative

PLATE 68
Frank Mason Good
British (dates unknown)
The Great Pyramid and Sphinx, 1873
Albumen print from glass negative

PLATE 69
Frank Mason Good
British (dates unknown)
Shipping on the Banks of the Nile, 1873
Albumen print from glass negative

PLATE 70
Frank Mason Good
British (dates unknown)
Tombs of the Mamelukes, Cairo, 1873
Albumen print from glass negative

PLATE 71
Frank Mason Good
British (dates unknown)
Boys Swimming in the Nile, 1873
Albumen print from glass negative

PLATE 72
Henri Béchard
French (dates unknown)
Dung Sellers, Cairo, 1880's
Albumen print from glass negative

PLATE 73
Henri Béchard
French (dates unknown)
Man with Woman on Donkey, 1880's
Albumen print from glass negative

120

N.º 23. Femme arabe   Béchard

PLATE 74
Henri Béchard
French (dates unknown)
Arab Woman, 1870's
Albumen print from glass negative

PLATE 75
Henri Béchard
French (dates unknown)
Cane Seller, 1880's
Albumen print from glass negative

Nº 19. Cheik Sadad / Descendant de Mahomet.   Béchad

PLATE 76
Henri Béchard
French (dates unknown)
Sheik Sadad, 1870's
Albumen print from glass negative

PLATE 77
Henri Béchard
French (dates unknown)
Orange Sellers, 1870's
Albumen print from glass negative

PLATE 78
Henri Béchard
French (dates unknown)
Arab Chanteuse, 1870's
Albumen print from glass negative

PLATE 79
Adolphe Braun
French (1812–1877)
Philae, 1869
Carbon print from glass negative

PLATE 80
Hippolyte Délié et Émile Béchard
French (dates unknown, active 1869–1890)
Plate #23, Civil Monuments, 1872
from the Bulak Museum Album, Cairo
Albumen print from glass negative

PLATE 81
Hippolyte Délié et Émile Béchard
French (dates unknown, active 1869–1890)
Plate #37, Historic Monuments, 1872
from the Bulak Museum Album, Cairo
Albumen print from glass negative

PLATE 82
Hippolyte Délié et Émile Béchard
French (dates unknown, active 1869–1890)
Plate #15, Historic Monuments, 1872
from the Bulak Museum Album, Cairo
Albumen print from glass negative

PLATE 83
J. Pascal Sebah
Turkish (?–1890)
Yarn Spinners, 1870's
Albumen print from glass negative

158. Femme fellah et son enfant.   P. Sébah phot.

PLATE 84
J. Pascal Sebah
Turkish (?–1890)
Fellah (Peasant) Woman and her Child, 1870's
Albumen print from glass negative

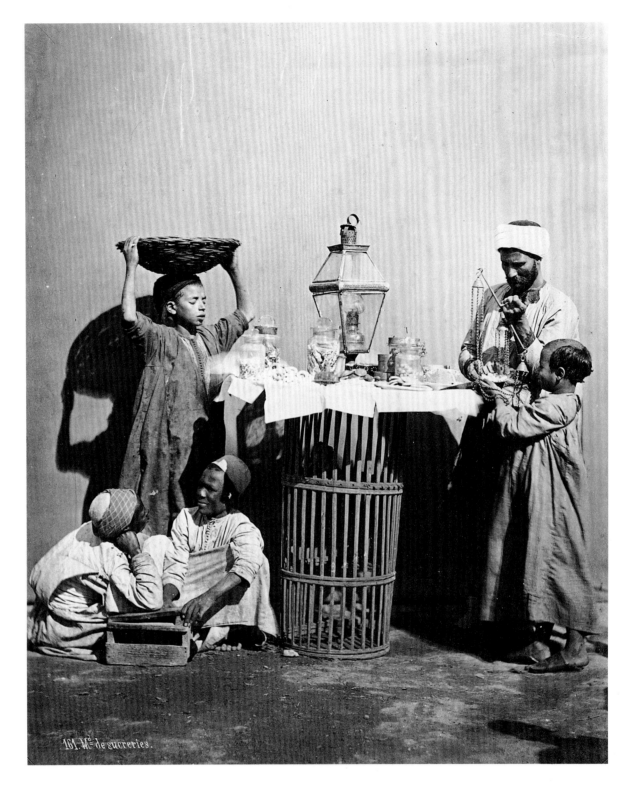

161. M^{de} de sucreries.

PLATE 85
J. Pascal Sebah
Turkish (?–1890)
Sweet Sellers, Cairo, 1870's
Albumen print from glass negative

PLATE 86
J. Pascal Sebah
Turkish (?–1890)
Water Carriers, Cairo, 1870's
Albumen print from glass negative

PLATE 87
J. Pascal Sebah
Turkish (?–1890)
Scottish Soldiers Visiting the Sphinx, 1880's
Albumen print from glass negative

PLATE 88
Carlo Naya
Italian (1816–1882)
Portrait of a Woman, 1876
Albumen print from glass negative

PLATE 89
Carlo Naya & Otto Schoefft
Italian (1816–1882) and Austrian (dates unknown)
"Negress" from *Le Caire Pittoresque*, 1876
Carbon (?) print from glass negative

PLATE 90
Carlo Naya & Otto Schoefft
Italian (1816–1882) and Austrian (dates unknown)
"Peasant Type" from *Le Caire Pittoresque*, 1876
Carbon (?) print from glass negative

No 242. Groupe de Chiens

PLATE 91
J. Pascal Sebah & Joaillier
Turkish (?–1890) and French? (dates unknown)
Pack of Dogs, Cairo, 1880's
Albumen print from glass negative

Ascension de Pyramide N°8

PLATE 92
Abdullah Frères
Turkish (dates unknown)
Ascension of the Pyramid, c. 1890
Albumen print from glass negative

PLATE 93
Abdullah Frères
Turkish (dates unknown)
Sphinx of Giza, 1880's
Albumen print from glass negative

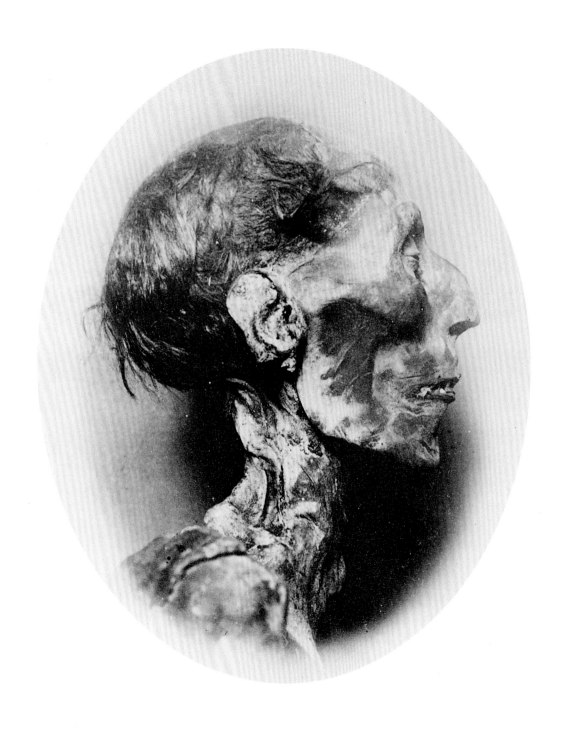

PLATE 94
Anonymous, attributed to Émile Brugsch
Mummy Head of Ramses II from the Bulak Museum, 1880's
Albumen print from glass negative

PLATE 95
Anonymous, attributed to Émile Brugsch
Mummy (standing) from the Bulak Museum, 1880's
Albumen print from glass negative

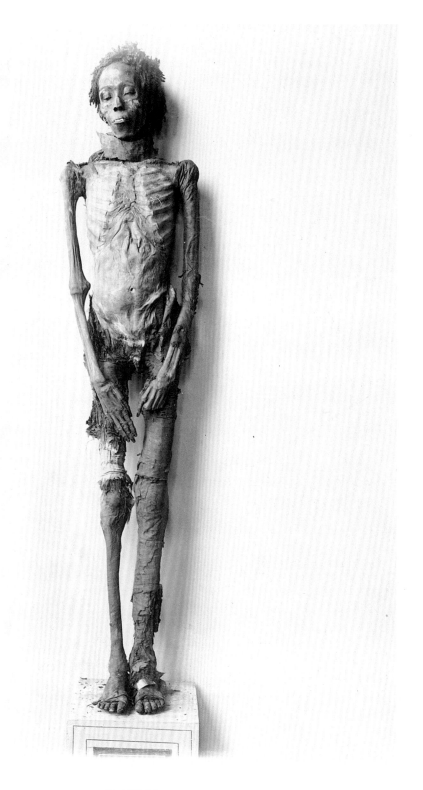

PLATE 96
Anonymous
Mummy of Mahinpra, 1890's
Gelatin silver print from glass negative

PLATE 97
Anonymous
Street of the Citadel, Cairo, c. 1858
Stereo albumen print from glass negative

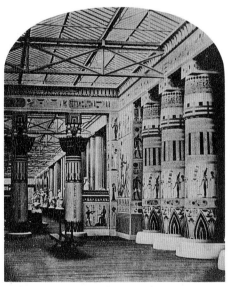

PLATE 98
Anonymous
The Egyptian Hall of Columns, Crystal Palace, London, 1853
Hand-painted stereo albumen print from glass negative

PLATE 99
Anonymous
The Egyptian Hall of Columns, Crystal Palace, London, 1853
Stereo albumen print from glass(?) negative

PLATE 100
Francis Frith
British (1822–1898)
Crocodile on Sand Bank, c. 1858
Stereo albumen print from glass negative

PLATE 101
Francis Frith
British (1822–1898)
Great Rock Temple of Abu Simbel, c. 1860
Stereo albumen print from glass negative

PLATE 102
Francis Frith
British (1822–1898)
Tombs of the Mamelukes
Stereo albumen print from glass negative

PLATE 103
C. E. Goodman
Nationality, dates unknown (active 1858)
Tombs of the Mamelukes, 1858
Stereo albumen print from glass negative

PLATE 104
Robert Murray (attributed)
British (dates unknown)
Two Men with Horse, 1863
Stereo albumen print

151

PLATE 105
Louis Rousseau
French (dates unknown)
Abdul Kerim Fade, Nubian, 1855
Albumen print from glass negative

PLATE 106
William Henry Fox Talbot (after Frith)
British (1800–1877)
Half of a Frith Stereo
Experimental photogravure process

May 19, 1798	Napoleon sails for Egypt with an army of conquest and a corps of scholars.
August 1, 1798	Nelson destroys the French fleet at the Bay of Aboukir.
June 1799	The Rosetta Stone is uncovered.
August 19, 1799	Napoleon abandons the Army of the Nile and returns to France.
1801	The French surrender Egypt to the British.
1802	Baron Dominique Vivant Denon publishes *Voyage dans la basse et la haute Égypte,* which becomes an instantaneous best seller.
1805	Mohammed-Ali Pasha, an Albanian Bey, consolidates rule in Egypt.
1809–1822	The mammoth *Description de l'Égypte* is published.
August 1, 1817	Belzoni opens the temple at Abu Simbel.
1818	The statue known as the Young Memnon (actually the head and shoulders of Ramses II) is displayed in the British Museum where it inspires Shelley's "Ozymandias."
1822	Jean François Champollion publishes his solution to the decipherment of hieroglyphics.
1830	An obelisk from Luxor is transported to Paris and set up in the Place de Concorde.
1832	American consulates open in Cairo and Alexandria.
1835	The first regular steamship service between Europe and Egypt (Marseilles to Alexandria) begins.
1835	John Murray publishes the first *Traveller's Handbook to Egypt.*
1837	Queen Victoria is crowned.
1838–39	David Roberts travels in Egypt and the Middle East making sketches for publication. The resultant six volumes of color lithographs are immensely popular.
January–August, 1839	Daguerre's process of producing a photographic image is announced to goverment, scientific, and artistic communities.
November, 1839	The first daguerreotypes are made in Egypt.
1846	The first scholarly study of hieroglyphs illustrated with photographs is published in London.
1847	Ibrahim Pasha succeeds his father as ruler of Egypt.
1848	Abbas Pasha succeeds Ibrahim.
1849	Maxime Du Camp with Gustave Flaubert undertakes the first government sponsored photographic survey of Egypt.

1849	Sir David Brewster develops the stereoscope, thus launching this popular parlor fixture of Victorian homes.
1851	Félix Teynard begins a photographic survey of the sites along the Nile.
1851	Frederic Scott Archer perfects the wet collodion on glass negative process.
1854	Said Pasha becomes ruler after the assassination of Abbas Pasha.
1854–56	Crimean War.
1855	The Alexandria-to-Cairo railroad is built.
1856	Said Pasha grants Ferdinand Lesseps a charter to build a canal across the Isthmus of Suez.
1856	Said Pasha forms the first Egyptian Antiquities Service and appoints Auguste Mariette (Mariette-Bey) director. He establishes the first museum of Egyptian Antiquities, in Egypt at Bulak in Cairo.
1863	Ismail Pasha succeeds Said Pasha.
1867	Mark Twain travels with the first American tour to the Mediterranean and Egypt. His letters and journals are published as *Innocents Abroad*.
October, 1869	The first package tour of Egypt lands at Alexandria.
November, 1869	Opening of the Suez Canal.
1872	Thomas Cook conducts the first tour group around the world.
1874	Jules Verne's *Around the World in Eighty Days* is published.
1875	Egypt's crushing national debt forces Ismail Pasha to sell Egypt's shares in the Suez Canal to Great Britain.
1875	Dry gelatin plates slowly begin to replace wet collodion glass negatives.
1876	John Cook opens a hotel at Luxor as a sanitarium.
1877–78	Cleopatra's Needle is removed from Alexandria and placed on the London Embankment.
1880	The obelisk of Thutmose III is removed from Alexandria and transported to its new site in New York's Central Park.
1881	Émile Brugsch discovers a cache of royal mummies.
1882	The Nationalist revolt of Arabi Pasha is put down by the British, and Sir Evelyn Baring (Lord Cromer) is named consul-general of Egypt.
1882	The Egypt Exploration Fund is started in London.
1888	The Kodak snapshot era begins.
1895	The first American chair in Egyptology is endowed at the University of Chicago.

APPENDIX B: PRINCIPAL BIOGRAPHIES

ABDULLAH FRÉRES (ABDULLAHIAN)

Turkish (dates unknown), active 1858–1880's

These three brothers of Armenian descent, Whichen, Kevork, and Hovsep, became interested in art early in their lives. Kevork studied painting in Venice; Whichen crafted ivory portrait miniatures in Constantinople. They assisted the German chemist Rabach in his Constantinople photo studio and laboratory from 1856–58. In 1858, Rabach returned to Germany and the brothers relocated the studio to Rue de Pera and renamed it "Abdullah Brothers." The Sultans Abdul Aziz and Abdul Hamid named the brothers official photographers of the court in 1862. To please the Sultan, the brothers (originally Abdullahian) probably changed their name and converted to Islam at this time.

They produced a major work documenting the Ottoman Empire and received eight orders of merit and three medals from the Ottoman Sultans and others. The brothers sold the family business to Sebah & Joaillier in 1899.

BEATO, ANTONIO

Italian, naturalized British citizen (c. 1825–1903), active late 1850's

Antonio was one of Egypt's most active photographers, leaving at the time of his death more than fifteen hundred negatives of varying dimensions, covering many aspects of Egyptian life. His career, which lasted nearly forty years, may have been inspired by a meeting he and his brother Felix had with photographer James Robertson in the early 1850s in Malta. Robertson later married their sister, Maria Matilde.

In the company that was established by his brother and Robertson—Robertson, Beato, and Co.—Antonio may have been the "Co." However, the two brothers did work independently, and Antonio claimed no public credit for his brother's accidental invention of a four-second exposure process.

Antonio's studio was originally established in Cairo in 1862 after Antonio returned from a fifteen-month Indian excursion. Later he relocated to Luxor from 1870 until his death. He used various formats (30x40, 24x30, and 18x24 cm) and also produced stereo photographs and cartes de visite. After his death the entire studio/house and all photographs, negatives, and equipment were offered for sale by his widow for fifty thousand francs. Gaston Maspero of the Bulak Museum purchased part of the collection.

BEATO, FELIX

Italian, naturalized British citizen (c. 1830–1906?), active 1857–?

Felix Beato made his photographs of Egypt in partnership with James Robertson, whom he met in the early 1850's in Malta. Their association continued through 1857, during which time they documented Constantinople, Athens, the Crimea, Egypt, Palestine, and India. Beato and Robertson are best known for photographs documenting the Indian Mutiny and its aftermath. Felix Beato is also known for his chemical experimentation, which reportedly allowed exposure time on albumen prints to be reduced to four seconds. Beato traveled and photographed extensively in Japan, producing hundreds of ethnographic portraits and genre scenes.

BÉCHARD, HENRI
French (dates unknown), active 1869–1880's

Béchard is known for high-quality images shot from unusual angles. His photographic studio was situated in Cairo in the Ezbekia Garden district. There is evidence that Béchard and the prolific Turkish photographer Sebah exchanged or purchased photographs from one another.

Béchard is noted for his fresh takes on and exciting presentation of common sites like the pyramids. The photographer's personal involvement with his subjects and their customs becomes remarkably apparent in his studies of costumes and people. In 1888, Béchard and A. Palmieri published his photographs as photogravures in *L'Égypte et la Nubie*.

BEDFORD, FRANCIS
British (1816–1894), active 1862

Before he began practicing photography in the early 1850's, Francis Bedford enjoyed a career as an architect and lithographer. After taking up photography in 1853, it was not long before he became known for exquisite photographs of church architecture. He traveled throughout the British Isles in the late 1850's making large format view photographs. In 1861, he was the first photographer to utilize electric light successfully in the printing process.

Bedford was selected by Queen Victoria in 1862 to accompany Edward, Prince of Wales, on his Middle Eastern Tour in order to document the royal expedition. During the journey, Bedford was occasionally assisted by Prince Alfred.

On March 3, 1862, Bedford took his first photo in Cairo. He returned home four months later with 210 negatives. One hundred and seventy-two of the prints were exhibited in a Bond Street gallery, and a set of 163 prints was published in 1863, many of holy sites previously unphotographed. The prints were highly praised by the *Art Journal* and the general public; they were later made available for purchase in smaller collections. *The Holy Land, Egypt, Constantinople, Athens, etc.*, with 48 reduced prints and a text by W. M. Thompson, was published by Day & Son in 1867.

BENECKE, ERNEST
French (dates unknown), active 1851–1858

Little is known of the French photographer who signed his prints E. Benecke, although he may have been a banker active in the Middle East during the 1850's. Prints by Benecke are quite rare, among them some of the earliest photographs of the people of the region. Five Benecke calotypes were published in three albums by Blanquart-Évrard, the photographic printer and publisher: one print appeared in *Album photographique de l'Artiste et de l'Amateur* (1851–1852); *Études photographiques* (1853) contains three Benecke prints; and *Varietés photographiques* (1853–1854) has one print by Benecke.

BONFILS, ADRIEN
French (1861–1928), active 1878–1895

BONFILS, FÉLIX
French (1831–1885), active 1867–81

BONFILS, MARIE-LYDIE CABANIS
French (1837–1918), active 1867–1916

Félix Bonfils, his wife, Marie-Lydie, and their son, Adrien, established the photographic studio of La Maison Bonfils in 1867 in Beirut. Félix had first visited Lebanon with French expeditionary forces in 1860 and was so impressed by the beauty and salubrious climate of the country that he and his wife later moved there for their son's health.

In only four years, the family and numerous assistants produced 15,000 photographic prints of Egypt, Palestine, Syria, and Greece, in addition to 9,000 stereoscopic views. Over the several decades in which the studio was in operation it expanded to branches in Jerusalem, Baalbek, Alexandria, and Cairo; tens of thousands of prints and lantern slides were generated. As clever at marketing techniques as at photographic ones, the Bonfils' works became known all over the world. Karl Baedeker's widely used travel guidebook of 1894 noted that there were three photographic dealers of note in Beirut: Bonfils, Dumas, and Guarelli; an asterisk beside Bonfils' name appeared as a mark of commendation.

The Maison Bonfils was also known for commercial portrait photography, and Marie-Lydie played a large role in photographing female subjects. The authenticity of the costumes and settings for these portraits should be questioned, because their purpose was not to document cultural reality, but to create an exotic scene. Fake props were used, such as papier-mâche rocks, and people were reportedly paid to pose in various costumes.

When Félix died in 1885, the firm was managed by his son Adrien. When Adrien left the family business in 1895 to open a hotel, Marie-Lydie maintained the company and kept photographing until she was evacuated by the United States Navy in 1916.

BRAUN, ADOLPHE
French (1812–1877), active 1869

Adolphe Braun, born in Besançon, started his professional career as a draftsman for the textile firm Dollfus-Meigs in Mullhouse. In 1853 he used photography to make a catalogue of flowers for artists to use in their compositions. He opened a photographic studio in Dornach, Alsace, in 1854.

His was one of only two photographic firms officially invited to the historic opening of the Suez Canal in 1869. His firm's catalogue, published immediately following, included an assortment of views of Cairo and its monuments taken at the time, but not a single print of the Canal. His son Gaston, also a photographer, accompanied him on some of his journeys and is sometimes credited with the Egyptian photographs.

HENRY CAMMAS
French (1813–?), active 1860's

Cammas was a member of the French Photographic Society and a corresponding member of the Egyptian Institute of Cairo, a society devoted to Egyptological studies. His Egyptian studies were advanced by his friendship with Mr. Koenig, the Alsatian tutor of Said Pasha, son and sucessor of Mohammed Ali. When Said Pasha came to the throne in 1854, Koenig became his principal advisor and undoubtedly facilitated Cammas' work in Egypt. Cammas and André Le Fèvre traveled in Egypt in 1860, during which time Cammas made over one hundred large-format waxed paper negatives of archaeological sites. Eighty-six prints were published with a text by Le Fèvre, *La Vallée du Nil* (1862). Although Cammas was one of the last photographers to use waxed paper negatives extensively in Egypt (the wet glass collodion technique with its superior detail had become the process of choice), his work was exhibited to widespread praise at the 1862 and 1867 Universal Expositions. Almost two decades later, Cammas' photographs were still cited as examples of the scientific application of photography.

DE CLERCQ, LOUIS
French (1836–1901), active 1859–1860

The wealthy young amateur Louis De Clercq was known to be interested in photography and archaeology. When, in 1859, Emmanuel-Guillaume Rey, the pre-eminent historian of the Crusades, was commissioned by the Ministry of Public Instruction to survey Crusader architecture in Syria and Asia Minor, De Clercq was invited to accompany him to assist with the photography of the sites. After fulfilling his obligation to Rey, De Clercq continued his photographic exploration of Syria and the Holy Land, moved on to Egypt, and returned to Europe through Spain. He published a selection of two hundred and twenty-two albumen prints from his travels, in six volumes titled *Voyage en Orient*, 1859–1860 (occasionally cited as five volumes because Vols. III & IV, "Views of Jerusalem" and "The Stations of the Cross," are sometimes bound together).

De Clercq used the paper negative process, and his work is distinguished by the number of large, multi-negative panoramas he included. During his first trip to the East, he collected objects as well as photographic subjects. Although on subsequent travels he continued building a choice collection of antiquities, which ultimately was donated to the Louvre, he made no further photographs.

DÉLIÉ, HIPPOLYTE, AND ÉMILE BÉCHARD
French (dates unknown), active 1869–1890

Délié and Béchard became partners after Délié arrived in Cairo, about the time of the opening of the Suez Canal in 1869. Both had worked in commercial photography prior to their association. Délié's travel views had been published as woodcuts in the weekly *Le Tour Du Monde*. Little is known of Béchard, who may have been related to Henri Béchard and trained by him. Together they prepared the photographs for the beautifully printed *Album du Musée Boulaq: Photographie par Délié et Béchard, avec texte explicatif par Auguste Mariette Bey* (Cairo,1872), a photographic survey of the archaeological treasures in the antiquities museum at Cairo.

Although Délié and Béchard dissolved their partnership in the 1870's, both continued to work in Egypt as commercial photographers. Délié joined the French Photographic Society in 1876 and was awarded a bronze medal at the Paris Universal Exposition of 1878. Émile Béchard was recognized with a gold medal at the same exposition.

MAXIME DU CAMP
French (1822–1894), active 1849–1851

Maxime Du Camp, a writer and fashionable man-about-town in 1840's Paris, had established a reputation as a traveler with books he had published about his journeys in North Africa and along the Breton coast. He used his family connections to obtain a government commission to travel throughout Egypt, Syria, and Palestine. He took lessons in photography from Le Gray and presented himself to the Académie des Inscriptions et Belles-Lettres for their instructions on which sites and monuments they would particularly like to have photographed. He also made plaster casts of inscriptions and carvings at the Academy's request.

Du Camp's journals and subsequent books, such as *Le Nil* (1855), and the letters and travel notes of his companion Gustave Flaubert, provide one of the most complete accounts of the European experience of Middle Eastern travel and of the daunting enterprise of making photographs during the early years of photography. Although Du Camp returned with over 200 negatives, his work is primarily known by the 125 images printed by Blanquart-Évrard and published with Du Camp's text by Gide et Baudry as *Égypte, Nubie, Palestine, et Syrie* (1852), the first photographically illustrated travel book. Du Camp was awarded the Legion of Honor in 1852 for his accomplishments during his travels in the East. His interest in photography did not outlast his travels: he divested himself of all of his photographic apparatus in Beirut.

FRITH, FRANCIS
English (1822–1898), active 1856–60

Francis Frith was the most well-known photographer in the nineteenth century who traveled to the Middle East. He used the wet collodion glass plate negative process and worked in multiple formats, including the 16 x 20" mammoth plate format. He visited Egypt twice on his three excursions to the Middle East, first in 1856–57 and later in 1859–60. His highly acclaimed stereoscopic views and stereo slides were made and distributed by Negretti & Zambra and his large loose prints by Thomas Agnew and Sons.

Frith, originally in the wholesale grocery and printing business, took up photography in the early 1850's. After his first trip to Egypt, he published *Egypt and Palestine Photographed and Described by Francis Frith* (London: J.S. Virtue, 1858–60). The two-volume book contained seventy-six albumen prints, issued serially in twenty-five parts. Other publications were to follow.

Frith's commercial photography business thrived. By 1860 he owned thousands of images. His catalogue of 1876 advertised over four thousand images and included 350 views of the Middle East.

GOOD, FRANK MASON
British (dates unknown), active 1860's–1880's

Good's photographic career probably began in the early 1860's, shortly before he joined the Photographic Society of London in 1864. A commercial view photographer known for his landscapes of the Isle of Wight, he was commissioned by Frances Frith to photograph in Egypt in 1867. Although unattributed, much of his work from this trip appeared in Frith's catalogues. He traveled to Egypt again in 1873, and again used the wet collodion glass negative technique which he had praised in an article in *The Photographic Journal*

(15 February 1873) as providing the clearest detail in deep shadows. Photographs from both trips were published as *Glimpses of the Holy Land* (1880). Good also made stereo views of Egypt which were published by Léon and Lévy of Paris.

GOODMAN, C. E.
Nationality and dates unknown, active 1858

All that is known about Goodman is that he visited Egypt in 1858, when he produced a set of stereographs. He may have used the wet collodion process.

GREENE, JOHN BEASLEY
American (1832–1856), active 1853–1856

Greene, the French-born son of an American banking family in Paris, was a founding member of the French Photographic Society and a student of Gustave Le Gray. He also belonged to the Société Orientale and the Société Asiatique, both learned societies devoted to Eastern studies. The nineteen-year-old's combined interests led him to Egypt in the fall of 1853 to photograph the land and record its mounuments and inscriptions. Upon his return to Paris in 1854, Blanquart-Évrard published ninety-four of his salt-paper prints as *Le Nil, monuments, paysages, explorations photographiques par J. B. Greene*. Greene's photographs are evenly divided between the archaeologist's meticulous record of fragmentary texts and the poetic evocation of landscape one would expect from a student of Le Gray. He returned to Egypt later the same year with permission to conduct his own excavations at Medinet-Habu. He documented the successive stages of that excavation with photographs, which he deposited at the Institute of France, and published a monograph, *Fouilles éxecutées à Thebes dans l'année 1855,* reporting his results. His third expedition ended in his death in Egypt in November 1856. Greene's negatives went to fellow photographer and Egyptologist Théodule Dévéria and are now in the collection of the Musée d'Orsay.

HAMMERSCHMIDT, W.
German (dates unknown), active c. 1860 on.

Perhaps one of the best resident photographers of Egypt, W. Hammerschmidt opened a shop selling photographs and photographic materials in Cairo around 1860 or earlier. Cammas reportedly bought supplies from him. At the exhibition of the Société Française de Photographie in 1861 he showed ten views taken in Egypt. One year later he became a member of the Société and in 1863 he exhibited more Egyptian works.

A comparison of similarities in Hammerschmidt's and Francis Frith's work places the bulk of Hammerschmidt's photography of Egypt between 1859 and 1869. In the desert outside Cairo, after being warned by Muslim pilgrims on their way to Mecca not to take photographs, Hammerschmidt was shot and wounded. After a brief return home to Berlin, Hammerschmidt came back to Cairo, and in 1869 photographed the interiors of St. Sepulchre in Jerusalem, using solar reflectors to bring previously unphotographed surfaces to light .

JOAILLIER (SEE J. PASCAL SEBAH)

LE GRAY, GUSTAVE
French (1820–1882), active 1848–1882

Gustave Le Gray, a student in the atelier of the painter Delaroche, was the pre-eminent photographic experimenter and teacher in Paris in the 1850's, as well as a practicing photographer devoted to the artistic possiblities of the medium. He probably taught Cammas, Du Camp, De Clercq, Greene, and Teynard, of the photographers cited in this text.

By 1860, when Le Gray departed France with a yachting party led by Alexander Dumas on a tour of the Mediterranean, he had established a significant reputation throughout Europe. Le Gray soon left Dumas' party and traveled throughout the Middle East, arriving finally in Egypt. He had in Paris photographed Said Pasha, the viceroy of Egypt, and he quickly established a connection with the Egyptian court. Le Gray remained in Egypt, first in Alexandria and then in Cairo, working as a commercial photographer and as drawing and painting instructor to the court. He died in Egypt in 1882.

McDONALD, SERGEANT JAMES

British (dates unknown), active 1858–1869

James McDonald was trained in photography at the School of Royal Engineers in Chatham, where his instructor was most likely Captain W. Abney, a traveler in India and Egypt. From 1864 to 1865 he was assigned to survey Palestine with Charles W. Wilson. McDonald's phototgraphs were published in the *Ordnance Survey of Jerusalem* (London, 1865).

On a second trip with Wilson, this time the Sinai peninsula in 1868, McDonald made at least 264 photographs, 153 of which were published in a three-volume survey. The Ordnance Survey Office in South Hampton also sold individual photographs (portrait and type studies) not included in the published volumes. McDonald's survey of the Sinai is noted as one of the most comprehensive surveys of the area. In 1869 McDonald was promoted to master sergeant and appointed one of two managers of the Photographic Office of the Royal Engineers' Establishment.

MURRAY, ROBERT

British (dates unknown), active 1852 through 1860's

Robert Murray was chief engineer to Mohammad-Ali, viceroy of Egypt. Although he made photos over the course of at least ten years and exhibited them, examples of his work are quite rare. Ten exist in the Royal Academy of Fine Arts in Copenhagen and one other, a photozincograph, is housed in the Smithsonian Institution in Washington, D.C.

NAYA, CARLO

Italian (1816–1882), active 1876

Carlo Naya and his brother Giovanni, following the wishes of their wealthy father, studied jurisprudence at the University of Pisa. After their father's death they used their inheritance to visit Asia and North Africa. Giovanni died suddenly in Constantinople in 1857. Upon returning home and settling in Venice, Carlo Naya opened a photography studio in partnership with Otto Schoefft. In the 1870's he became a member of the Société Française de Photographie and was appointed King Victor Emmanuel's photographer.

He constructed genre scenes for photographs in his native Italy and used the same methods when he traveled to Egypt in 1876. His talent for staging and design and knowledge of art history enabled him to create tableaux that were opulently realistic. His photographs were published as etchings or wood engravings accompanying written texts on travel in the Orient.

ROBERTSON, JAMES

British (1813–1882?), active 1850's

Robertson is believed to have been the chief engraver at the Imperial Mint in Constantinople. There is no record of how he became interested in photography, but his signed photographs made near Constantinople are dated 1854. By the end of 1854 his photographs were regularly reproduced in *The Illustrated London News*. In late 1855 he became associated with the Beato brothers when he married their sister. That same year he took many photographs during the Crimean War and achieved some reknown when they were exhibited with those of Roger Fenton. His association with Felix Beato began in 1857 when Robertson was appointed the official photographer to the British Army in India and set off for his new post with his brother-in-law. They photographed in Egypt and Palestine on their way to India and covered the aftermath of the Indian Mutiny once there. The photographs made under their partnership are signed "Robertson and Beato" or "Robertson Beato et Cie." Their partnership was probably dissolved at the end of their tour of duty in India.

LOUIS ROUSSEAU

French(dates unknown), active 1850's

Rousseau was a naturalist and photographer who collaborated with Théodule Dévéria on one of the first scientific publications illustrated with photographs, *Photographie zoologique ou représentation des animaux râres des collections du Musée d'histoire naturelle* (Paris, 1853). A notice in *La Lumière* of 16 June 1855 recorded the recent arrival of an Egyptian frigate carrying a young female hippopotamus as a gift from Halem-Pasha, brother of the viceroy of Egypt, to Napoleon III. The notice went on to advertise Rousseau's success at the

Museum of Natural History in obtaining "three good prints which represent each of two Nubians accompanying the beast, twenty and twenty-eight years of age, and the beast itself."

SCHOEFFT, OTTO
Austrian (dates unknown), active 1860's–1890's

A professional photographer in Cairo, Otto Schoefft was mentioned in Baedeker's *Egypt: Handbook for Travelers* (1885). Schoefft's first partnership was with Carlo Naya in Italy in 1865. Once in Egypt he began to collaborate with Schier, a fellow Austrian in Alexandria. Although discussed in many publications of the period (Baedeker compliments Schoefft on his attractive studio backgrounds for groups of native people and his desert landscapes), relatively few of Schoefft's photographs are known.

SEBAH, J. PASCAL
Turkish (?–1890), active 1860's–1870's

Owner of a large commercial studio of photography in Constantinople opened in 1868, Sebah's signed photographs appeared in nearly every collaborative album between the 1870's and 1890's. Joaillier entered into partnership with Sebah in the company which was advertised on the reverse of some cartes de visite as El Chark or "The Orient." Some prints were signed with both of their names, others by Sebah alone.

Sebah did not limit himself to one format, but produced stereo cards, cartes de visite, large-format views, and panoramas. His photos were regularly used as scientific illustrations in Orientalist publications.

Signed works are so numerous and varied that scholars suspect they may not all be the work of one man. He probably had assistants doing photography as the business grew. Sebah is also known to have shared negatives with Béchard; whether the negatives were actually exchanged or borrowed is not known. Sebah won a silver medal at the Exposition Universelle of 1878 for his photographs of Egypt, especially his portraits of the Nubian desert tribes.

SCHRANZ, ANTON
Maltese (1801–?), active 1852–54

Although he seems to have traveled widely in the Middle East in the 1840's, Anton Schranz's career in photography appears to have begun about ten years later. His work mainly consists of views of Cairo, its monuments, and architecture. He heavily retouched his photographs to bring out details and add clouds in the skies.

TEYNARD, FÉLIX
French (1817–1892), active 1851–52

Trained as a civil engineer, Félix Teynard was the son of an old and privileged family. He grew up in Grenoble, a center for Egyptological studies in the early nineteenth century. It seems likely that Teynard learned photography in order to create a photographic version of the *Description de l'Égypte*. On 7 December 1851 he received a passport in Cairo to travel up the Nile, and set out to photograph the sites reproduced in the *Description* and in a later publication of Nubian antiquities by the architect Gau. Upon his return, a sumptuous set of 160 salt-paper prints was published in thirty-two installments between 1853 and 1858 by Goupil et Cie as *Égypte et Nubie*. Its price of one thousand gold francs, which made it the most expensive photographically illustrated book of the time, may be the reason so few copies are known to exist.

TREMAUX, PIERRE
French (1818–?), active 1853–1868

The architect Pierre Tremaux was trained at the École des Beaux-Arts, where he was awarded a second place in the Prix de Rome of 1845. A member of both the Académie des Beaux-Arts and the Société de Géographie, Tremaux combined interests in architecture and geography, and is primarily known for a massive three-part publication on the architecture of Africa and Asia Minor: Part I, *Voyage au*

Soudan oriental et dans l'Afrique septentrionale exécutés de 1847 à 1854 (1852–1854); Part II, *Une parallèle des édifices anciens et modernes du continent africain* (1861); Part III, *Exploration archéologique en Asia mineur* (1862–1868).

Tremaux first traveled to North Africa and Egypt in 1847–1848. Lithographs based on his drawings of the region began to appear in 1852 and brought Tremaux government support for a second expedition to the region, during which he made calotypes (1853–1854). His photographic knowledge, no doubt acquired quickly between expeditions, was inadequate to the technical challenge, and the photographic prints began to deteriorate quickly. He sent the following apologetic note to subscribers: "Since the photographs are not sufficiently impervious to the effects of light and other agents to guarantee the certainty of their lasting for the whole production of the work, they will be reproduced by lithography in the future. The difficult circumstances under which they were produced has necessarily caused their mediocrity." For the third part of the series, Tremaux used Poitevin's photolithography process. His work was recognized with the Legion of Honor in 1864 by Napoleon III.

SOURCES CONSULTED

Chevedden, Paul E. *The Photographic Heritage of the Middle East.* Malibu: Undena Publications, 1981.

Fabian, Rainer, and Hans-Christian Adam, *Egypt: Lion-Hearted Journey to the Temples of the Nile, Masters of Early Travel Photography.* New York, Paris: The Vendome Press, 1983.

Haworth-Booth, Mark. *The Golden Age of British Photography, 1839–1900.* New York: Aperture, 1984.

Jammes, André, and Eugenia Parry Janis. *The Art of French Calotype with a Critical Dictionary of Photographers, 1845–1870.* Princeton: Princeton University Press, 1983.

Jammes, Marie-Thérèse, and André. "Egypt in Flaubert's Time: The First Photographers, 1839–1860." *Aperture* 78 (1977): 62–77.

Janis, Eugenia Parry. *The Photography of Gustave Le Gray.* Chicago: University of Chicago Press, 1987.

Marbot, Bernard. *Regards sur la Photographie en France au XIXe siècle.* With an essay by Weston Naef. Paris: Berger Levrault, 1980.

Naef, Weston, and Lucien Goldschmidt. *The Truthful Lens: A Survey of the Photographically Illustrated Book, 1844–1914.* New York: The Grolier Club, 1980.

Perez, Nissan. *Focus East: Early Photography in the Near East, 1839–1885.* New York: Abrams, 1988.

Szegedy-Maszak, Andrew. "Sun and Stone: Images of Ancient Heroic Times." *Archaeology* 41, no. 4 (1988): 20–31.

Thomas, Ritchie. "Some 19th Century Photographers in Syria, Palestine and Egypt." *History of Photography* 3, no. 2 (1979): 157–166.

Michael G. Wilson

PLATE 2
Du Camp traveled with Gustave Flaubert throught Egypt and the Near East from 1849 to 1851. Although Du Camp was a novelist, poet, journalist, and soldier, rather than a photographer, he was the first person to make a comprehensive survey of Egyptian monuments. The resulting work of 125 original photographs *Égypt, Nubie, Palestine, et Syrie* (1852) was the first major book illustrated with photographs published in France. The image depicted here is one of a pair of monoliths in the plain of Thebes. (see Frith, p. 90 and Greene, p. 67).

PLATE 3
Here Hadiji, dressed only in his loin cloth, stands before ruins which Du Camp suggests are those of Ozymandias, the mythical king from Shelley's poem.

PLATE 4
Until this time most Europeans had only seen hieroglyphics reproduced as engravings and lithographs, but in Du Camp's photograph the stone becomes real, the inscriptions palpable.

PLATE 5
Only the structural body of this ancient temple survives, and the viewer is left to speculate on the splendor of its plundered facade. Like a mythical guide to the underworld, the figure in white waits on the darkened threshold.

PLATE 6
To the eyes of French painters (and viewers) used to the tree-filled landscapes of their native country, this Egyptian variation must have seemed exotic indeed.

PLATE 7
Benecke was one of the first who took an interest in photographing Egypt's native population. Little is known of Benecke's life, and his work is rare.

PLATE 8
Félix Teynard was an engineer who traveled through Egypt in 1851 and 1852. His surviving work consists of 162 photographs, 160 of which were published in installments from 1853 through 1858.

PLATE 9
Teynard had an extraordinary command of the waxed paper negative process, which he learned from the great Parisian photographer Gustave Le Gray. Even in this picture, made in the harshest lighting conditions, he is able to produce a print of broad tonal range.

PLATE 10
The prints from Teynard's books range in color from rose-pink to deep violet. Compare the color of this print with the next two.

PLATE 11
This print is unusual in that it was never mounted. It reveals the full extent of the original negative. The scribe marks indicate where the print was to be cropped for the published edition.

PLATE 12
The helmsman and a sailor from the boat which took Teynard up the Nile appear in these photographs; they are the only ones Teynard ever took of a human subject.

PLATE 14
Only a limited number of Teynard books illustrated with original photographs were produced, no doubt because of their price. At 1,000 gold francs, they were twice as expensive as Du Camp's.

PLATE 15
Pierre Tremaux's enigmatic studies are among the earliest photographs of Egyptian people. Unfortunately his lack of command of photographic technique caused many of his images to fade.

PLATE 16
Greene was an amateur archaeologist and a singular talent; his pictures evoke a secret realm of riddle and romance.

PLATE 17
This photograph is ostensibly about the inscriptions on the temple wall, but the empty, black doorway dominates the composition, offering a mysterious gateway to the past. Who and what lies buried within?

PLATE 18
The majestic statue of a female goddess is hidden in the deep shadows of the temple. On the wall behind, a recent visitor has inscribed ghost-like graffiti.

PLATE 19
Greene's impression of the second cataract is more a memory than a documentary landscape. He uses the limitations of the paper negative to his advantage, creating a poetic, almost ethereal, image.

PLATE 20
Greene's personal vision is evidenced by this unique view of the rear of the colossus. Greene isolates the monolith against an empty sky, focusing the viewer's attention on the inscription and the crack, which was said to sound a low, haunting tone when the wind blew through it.

PLATE 21
Murray, a British engineer working in Cairo, was the first local resident to photograph widely in Egypt. Although a 163-print portfolio of his images was published in London to critical acclaim, few of his images survive. To date, less than twenty have been inventoried.

PLATE 22
In the days before tourism to Southern Spain and North Africa became commonplace, even such a mundane subject as a cactus grove was an exotic sight to the European traveler.

PLATE 23
A view of a Cairo street by the photographer of *Cactus Grove*. Here the focus is not the antiquities of ancient civilizations, but the Moslem world of contemporary Egypt.

PLATE 24
Another view of the same Cairo street printed from a glass plate negative. A comparison of this image to the previous one highlights the difference between prints made from glass and paper negatives.

PLATE 25
Robertson and Beato were professional photographers residing in Turkey whose subjects included both contemporary life and ancient monuments. While much of their work from other countries survives, their Egyptian work is rare.

PLATE 26
Robertson and Beato used a secret dry plate albumen process to make their glass negatives. It was more convenient to use in the field than the wet plate collodion process used by their contemporaries, which required that the negatives be made and processed on location before they dried. However, later editions of these images show significant negative deterioration. Apparently, the albumen-coated glass plates were more fragile than collodion.

PLATE 27
This self-portrait captures Frith indulging in the early travelers' custom of shedding their frock coats and "going native."

PLATE 28
Frith participated in the popular, but frustrating, sport of hunting crocodiles. Like most of his contemporaries, he was unsuccessful. Comparing this picture with the stereograph (p. 147) of the identical subject reveals the same crocodile in both pictures at two different locations. Frith, more showman than scientist, toured with a stuffed crocodile.

PLATE 29
According to Frith: ". . . the accumulated sands of ages have buried this once magnificent pile to the capitals of the columns, and its stunted height strikes you as strangely disproportionate to the vastness of its other dimensions, and the immense size of the stones. It reminds you of some grand old giant buried to the shoulders—not dead yet, but overpowered and imprisoned by some potent spell—majestic in his helplessness. . . . It is aggravating to know, that a money-grubbing, sugar-baking pasha (Abbas) has split up and carried off many of these superb blocks to be used in the building of his sugar refineries, of which branch of trade, and many others, the pasha usurps a monopoly."

PLATE 30
Frith commented in detail about this image: "The view was taken during a storm, which may partly account for its great success. To this too is owing the weird aspect of the leafless tree to the left, which gives such great vigor to the picture. No human could have copied that strange network of branches, while representing them struggling with the storm wind of the desert. The utter absence of vegetation . . . gives an almost unearthly majesty to these scenes of the Arabian desert. Nature is here stripped of the beautiful colours and forms that elsewhere vary her surface, and reduced to the bare conditions of her oldest state."

PLATE 31
Frith favored Mount Horeb over Mount Serbal as the mountain where Moses was given the Ten Commandments. He came to this conclusion because the large open area at the foot of Horeb was sufficient to accommodate the large encampment of Israelites who accompanied Moses, while Mount Serbal had no such area.

PLATE 32
Frith was frustrated by the dilapidated state of the houses around the mosque, which made it difficult to find a favorable position from which to photograph: "Cairo . . . exhibits a multitide of grand and imposing objects, choked up with such as are mean, unseemly, and foul."

PLATE 33
This was Frith's favorite place. The boat pictured is his: "This boat costs our party thirty pounds per month, including the wages of the Rais and ten men . . . The pioneers of what is now the 'Nile excursion,' were accustomed to sink their boats for a few days, in order to rid them of unwelcome tenants; but the *dahabieh* now-a-days are smart and cleanly—often luxurious, some few having, besides excellent canteens, &c., very fair libraries of European books, and even pianofortes!" The black tent on the small boat in the center of the picture is Frith's portable darkroom.

PLATE 34
The looting and destruction at Karnak infuriated Frith: "I believe there is not now known to exist in Egypt a single statue or sphinx of movable proportions which is in any tolerable state of preservation. . . . Hundreds of these beautiful sculptures now enrich the museums and private collections of all Europe, but only the intelligent Egyptian traveler can fully appreciate their loss to Egypt. Methinks it were better that a few men who will be at the pains of seeking them in their legitimate places should enjoy them as they can only there be enjoyed, rather than that the hordes of careless people who throng the British museum even should smile thoughtlessly at their incongruous quaintness, and in England, their unintelligible grandeur."

PLATE 35
Frith observed: "The mosque of the Sultan Hasan is a very noble pile, towering above all the other edifices of Cairo. The disparity of its two minarets is, however, a drawback to its complete beauty." Frith goes on to recount that a third minaret, opposite the smaller one at the entrance, collapsed while under construction, killing all but a handful of some three hundred orphaned children. The construction was thereafter abandoned.

PLATES 36 and 37
Plate 36 is the most popular "Second View" included in the Frith albums. The inclined structures on the roof provided shade for the air shafts within the buildings.

   Plate 37 is a variant view that was published in a few of the Frith albums as the "Second View." It shows the relationship between the Pyramids and the city.

PLATE 38
Frith commented: "The Southern Stone Pyramid is the chief object in the view. Rising from the waves of sand, it presents a grand mass the strange form of which makes its size more apparent, though it lessens its symmetry."

PLATE 39
This is the only instance where Frith did not condemn the plunder of the ancient monuments: "It is a picturesque mass, of very irregular form, rising out of a mound made by its own ruins. The peasants have quarried it for building materials, and given it the rugged shape it now wears. We can scarcely regret their barbarism, which has varied the aspect of what must have long been a mere rounded pyramid, and produced these admirable contrasts of light and shade, and of rough and smooth surface."

PLATE 40
Frith on graffiti: "On the right shoulder of the colossus is the prenomen of Rameses II. On the head may be seen the barbarous inscriptions of modern travelers—instances of a mania as reprehensible as it is childish. It is to be hoped that the best-known names will be collected and published, in order that the consequent disgrace may deter others from earning the same notoriety."

PLATE 41
Frith did not completely accept the notion that this was the ruin referred to in Shelley's poem. "The temple was probably known to the ancients under the name of the Tomb of Osymandyas, which is described minutely by Diodorus in terms that to a large extent suit the probable plan and condition of the Ramesseum of that day. . . . 'But we may be allowed to question its having been a tomb, or having been erected by that monarch' (quoting Sir William Grandner)."

PLATE 42
This view was one of the two most popular of the city streets because this was one of the few places where the streets were not narrow and winding. Frith commented: "A map of Cairo is very curious, showing how entirely persons are mistaken who, seeing only the streets and lanes, imagine it to be a crowded city. All the best houses have courts—some very spacious—into which the principal apartments look; and although for the purposes of ventilation the plan may be imperfect, it is the only one suitable to the Eastern life."

PLATE 43
Frith took exception to the excavations at Thebes. Many of the objects destined for the museum at Cairo had found "their way into other collections." He was outraged by the Pasha's methods. "In some instances, noble masses of picturesque ruin have been blown to pieces, and removed without any idea of uncovering ojects of interest, but simply to clear space. . . . The hands employed are generally children, who are pressed from the adjoining villages. They carry out the dust in baskets upon their heads, and their movements are continually accelerated by 'taskmasters' armed with corbashes, or whips of hippopotamus hide, which are capable of inflicting a terrible stroke."

PLATE 44
This is the principal structure in the area east of Cairo known as the Tombs of the Mameluke Kings. Frith photographed extensively in the area in 1857-58, at the same time as the British photographer, Goodman (see p. 150), whose stereograph shows a photographer and his carriage waiting patiently for the photographer to finish his exposure. Other than the coincidence of time, there is no other reason to suspect the man in the picture is Frith, but the image does suggest how the well-outfitted photographer might have looked in the field.

PLATE 45
Frith comments on the small quarry near the Second Pyramid: "of this quarry we have very pleasant recollections, for we made it our home when first we visited the Pyramids. The partly blocked-up entrance, to the left of the view, made an excellent kitchen and shelter for the servants, while beyond was a spacious rocky hall, lighted by three apertures, which, with a canvas, could be divided into two rooms. . . . here we slept in the soft pure desert air, and when the howling of the jackals, most mournful of sounds, broke our rest, passed out and saw the full splendor of the desert sky, and the dark masses of the Pyramids rising sharply against its clear depths."

PLATE 46
In Frith's words: "The day and hour in a man's life upon which he first obtains a view of 'The Pyramids,' is a time to date from for many a year to come; he is approaching, as it were, the presence of an immortality which has mingled vaguely with his thoughts from very childhood, and has been to him unconsciously an essential and beautiful form, and the most majestic mystery ever created by man."

PLATE 47
Frith at his most dramatic, wrote: ". . . the dazzling sunlight . . . and as strong shade . . . the undulations of shifting sand, with here and there a mummy-pit, into which an unwary passer-by may easily fall, bring back to the mind every characterisitic of this striking view. The lesser features are not wanting to render it complete: there, in the foreground, is a human skull, and a little beyond it the skull of a sacred bull. It is unusual chance that brings them here: throughout the whole vast Necropolis the bones of men and of bulls and ibises are strewn around the mouths of the desecrated pits." In other variants of this image Frith has rearranged the skulls to improve the composition.

PLATE 48
For Frith the Great Pyramid was the definitive one by which all others were to be compared. He found the pyramids a wonderful subject for reflection and meditation. "They stand in the desert, away or apart from the homes of men, where none of the signs of life can take the soul from the contemplation of eternity."

PLATE 49
Frith was not impressed with Jerusalem. Artists in the past had portrayed the city much grander than it was, and he feared the British public would be disappointed by his photographs. In his book, Frith took a positive tone: "Here the first feeling is the satisfaction produced by confidence; and as with a much-loved face, such a truthful record is of more value than the most elaborately beautiful picture."

PLATE 50
De Clercq was the last major photographer to use the paper negative in Egypt. This view of a rectangular building surrounded by a white wall depicts the residence of the Viceroy. Compare this view of the same building by Teynard (p. 57), taken from the other side of the residence.

PLATE 51
This photograph is as much about the rhythm of time as it is about the ruins. Geological time is indicated by the great wave of sand breaking between the buildings. Architectural time is shown by the weathering facade. Circadian time is attested to by the movement of the shadows, and human time by the blurred figures.

PLATE 52
In this unique perspective of an often-photographed subject, we view the sphinx from a distance, dwarfed by the Great Pyramid. Compare this to the more conventional view by Frith (p. 93).

PLATE 53
Le Gray is the acknowledged master of the waxed paper negative process. He taught many important photographers, including Du Camp and Teynard. (Compare Teynard's view of the same location, p. 61.) In spite of his artistic achievements, Le Gray failed in business. He closed his studio in Paris in 1859 and all but abandoned photography. He settled in Cairo, where he died in 1882 following a fall from a horse.

PLATE 54
The barrage, in the style of a medieval European fortress, was intended to control flooding along the Nile. It proved ineffective due to seepage under its foundations and was razed in 1883 and rebuilt. Hammerschmidt is one of the first European professional photographers to settle permanently in Egypt. Although the date of his arrival is uncertain, Henry Cammas reports having purchased photographic material from Hammerschmidt's studio on his 1860 trip.

PLATE 55
Antonio Beato, the brother of Felix (of Robertson and Beato), spent virtually all his forty years as a professional photographer in Egypt. The images in the Terry Album date from his earliest work. This view of Cairo was taken from the same location as Frith's second views (pp. 83, 84), but shows more of the city on the right-hand side.

PLATE 56
This favorite view is enlivened by the European artist sketching under his umbrella in an otherwise unpopulated landscape.

PLATE 57
These Beato photographs were preserved in a well-documented travel album by an officer in the British Army. The ephemera in the album indicates that the photographs were purchased in the first two weeks of April 1864. It is unusual to find nineteenth-century photographs that can be dated so precisely.

PLATE 58
Bedford, one of the most prominent British photographers, was asked to accompany the Prince of Wales (later Edward VII) on a tour of the Near East. While his views are of the usual sights, he brings a fresh vision to these subjects. In this view he incorporates the Moslem minaret, echoing the shape of the half-buried figures before the gate, into a view of the ancient temple.

PLATE 59
The Temple of Philae is here seen in context with the river and the distant bank of the Nile. Bedford has chosen a location on the interior of the island, rather than the more common view from the landing on the river (see Frith, p. 80).

PLATE 61
From a wonderfully dynamic perspective, Bedford shows the temple being engulfed by sand. Mindful of the historic importance of his trip with the Prince of Wales, Bedford precisely inscribed each negative with the place, day, month, and year.

PLATE 62
In this study of light and shade, Bedford has waited for the moment when the light would illuminate the fallen columns to the left of the figures. Prince Alfred (brother of the Prince of Wales), an amateur photographer himself, assisted Bedford in making the pictures during the tour.

PLATE 63
McDonald was a Colour Sergeant in the Royal Engineers and a military photographer who accompanied Charles Wilson on an 1868 survey of the Sinai.

PLATE 65
McDonald's work offers a fine example of the technical excellence achieved with glass plate negatives and correctly processed albumen paper. Although not apparent at first glance, McDonald has placed several figures in the landscape to provide a perception of depth.

PLATE 66
The Bonfils family established one of the most prolific photographic studios in the Near East. The business originated in Lebanon in 1867 and lasted for fifty years. This view is typical of the "native study" pictures in which most of the people depicted were paid models.

PLATE 67
No tour of Cairo would be complete without a visit to the rug merchant. While this view was marketed as a keepsake for tourists, such photographs were also used by Orientalist painters as a reference for their backgrounds.

PLATE 68
Although Good's photographs are slightly smaller than those of his contemporaries, their exacting compositions were printed to the highest standards; each one is like a perfect gem. Their tone and value remain as rich as when they were first printed one hundred and twenty years ago.

PLATE 69
Good captures the hustle and bustle of a thriving shipping port. The Nile was an important trade route within Egypt, a fact often overlooked by early photographers who tended to focus their cameras on monuments and ruins.

PLATE 70
Here is another of Good's unique compositions. The lone figure in the foreground and the three in the middle-ground guide the eye beyond the tombs to the city. The unnatural erectness of the figures, which normally would be disconcerting, mimic the shapes of the minarets and thus serves to integrate and harmonize the composition.

PLATE 71
Young boys swimming in a river is a persistent theme in Victorian art. In this image Good attempts to set a European theme in a Nile setting.

PLATE 72
Béchard settled in Cairo to become one of the largest suppliers of genre studies. Unlike Bonfils, he photographed out of the studio with realistic backgrounds. European tourists were fascinated and repulsed by such occupations as the dung sellers depicted here. At home, this picture would be proof that the traveler's stories were not exaggerations.

PLATE 73
This simple subject is appealing both as an illustration of the protective demeanor of upper-class Moslem women when they ventured out into the public and as a depiction of the favored Victorian Biblical theme of the flight into Egypt.

PLATE 74
The woman pictured here is in purdah. Camouflaged under a shapeless dress, she is completely covered except for a bare, ring-bedecked foot which just protrudes from the edge of her skirt, lending an earthy exoticism to the picture.

PLATE 75
Béchard manages a noble and dignified portrait of a humble profession.

PLATE 76
Said to be a direct descendant of the Prophet, Sheik Sadad was one of the most photographed dignitaries in Cairo.

PLATE 77
Hardly the site of a fruit market where one would expect to see orange sellers, the models are no doubt posed. Thus, the picture has more in common with modern advertising images than ethnography. Yet, it is the very artificiality of the picture, with its emphasis on detail and lighting, which makes it successful.

PLATE 78
For the European tourist a masked woman invited attention and engendered speculation—an effect contrary to that intended.

PLATE 79
Braun took his Egyptian views on a trip to the inaugural ceremonies of the Suez Canal in 1869. His approach was aesthetic rather than documentary or archeological. In this view the Temple at Philae is relegated to the background in a landscape study of the Nile.

PLATE 83
Sebah's original studio was in Istanbul, but sometime in the 1870's he established a branch in Cairo. Judging from the vast number of surviving prints, he was the most prolific commercial photographer in Egypt. His primary product was genre and ethnographic studies for tourists.

PLATE 87
The British bombarded Alexandria in 1882, successfully suppressing a Nationalist revolt lead by the head of the Egyptian army, Arabi Pasha. Scottish soldiers, who were part of the occupation force, pose before the Sphinx.

PLATE 88
Naya, a Venetian photographer, produced a series of large portraits of "local types." While many such studies by commercial photographers were caricatures, Naya was a notable exception. Most of his images are sensitive and dignified studies of the local people.

PLATE 89
This portrait is one of the few incisive studies of Africans made by a nineteenth-century commercial photographer.

PLATE 90
This Naya portrait is more typical of the style of commercial tourist photographers. The glazed eyes and smoking cigarette are meant to convey the impression of a hashish addict. The caption suggests the sitter is a typical Cairo peasant.

PLATE 92
Ten years after Frith's first trip, the Pyramids were overrun with tourists. Mark Twain described his view of Cheops: "Insect men and women were creeping about its dizzy perches and one little black swarm were waving postage stamps from the airy summit. . . ."

PLATE 93
The Sphinx looks out of balance with the sand of centuries removed.

PLATE 94
The once great pharoah, builder of Abu Simbel, is revealed as a gaunt, leathery-skinned curiosity. The photograph is coolly scientific and objective, akin to a police mug shot. Maspero observed, upon first seeing the unwrapped face: "Somewhat unintelligent expression, slightly brutish perhaps, but haughty and firm of purpose."

PLATE 95
The royal mummies were discovered by Émile Brugsch in 1881. They were shipped to the Cairo Museum and were unwrapped in front of the Khedive of Egypt in May 1886.

PLATE 96
Another of the royals removed from his sarcophagus and propped up for his picture.

PLATE 105
This Nubian was identified as the man "who accompanied the female Hippopotamus in 1885."

Quotes are taken from Francis Frith's four volumes covering upper and lower Egypt, Sinai, and Jerusalem, printed in London by William MacKenzie, Paternoster Row, 1862.

SELECTED BIBLIOGRAPHY

History of Photography

Janis, Eugenia Parry, and André Jammes. *The Art of French Calotype.* Princeton: Princeton University Press, 1983.

Newhall, Beaumont. *The History of Photography: From 1839 to the Present,* 5th ed. Boston: Little, Brown and Co., 1988.

Rosenblum, Naomi. *A World History of Photography.* New York: Abbeville, 1984.

Photography in Egypt and the Middle East

Buckland, Gail, and Louis Vaczek. *Travelers in Ancient Lands: A Portrait of the Middle East, 1839–1919.* Boston: New York Graphic Society, 1981.

Bull, Deborah, and Donald Lorimer. *Up the Nile: A Photographic Excursion: Egypt 1839–1898.* New York: Clarkson N. Potter, 1979.

Jammes, Marie-Thérèse, and André Jammes. *En Égypte au temps de Flaubert, les premiers photographes 1839–1860.* Paris: Kodak-Pathé, 1976. Reissued in translation as "Egypt in Flaubert's Time: An Exhibition of the First Photographers, 1839–1860," *Aperture* 78 (1977): 62–77.

Monti, Nicolas. *Africa Then: Photographs 1840–1918.* London: Thames and Hudson, 1987.

Perez, Nisan. *Focus East: Early Photography in the Near East, 1839–1885.* New York: Abrams, 1988.

Individual Photographers

Gavin, Carney E. S. *The Image of the East: Nineteenth-Century Near Eastern Photographs by Bonfils.* Chicago: University of Chicago Press, 1982.

Howe, Kathleen. *Félix Teynard: Calotypes of Egypt, A Catalogue Raisonné.* New York: Kraus, Hershkowitz, and Weston, 1992.

Janis, Eugenia Parry. *Louis De Clercq: Voyage en Orient.* Cologne: Mayer and Mayer, 1989.

Van Haaften, Julia. *Egypt and the Holy Land in Historic Photographs: 77 Views by Francis Frith.* New York: Dover Publications, Inc., 1980.

History of Travel

Brendon, Piers. *Thomas Cook: 150 Years of Popular Tourism.* London: Secker and Warburg, 1991.

Leed, Eric. *The Mind of the Traveler: From Gilgamesh to Global Tourism.* New York: Basic Books, 1991.

Lowenthal, David. *The Past is a Foreign Country.* Cambridge: Cambridge University Press, 1985.

Swinglehurst, Edmund. *The Romantic Journey: The Story of Thomas Cook and Victorian Travel.* New York: Harper and Row, 1974.

Egypt as Destination

Clayton, Peter. *The Rediscovery of Ancient Egypt: Artists and Travelers in the 19th Century.* London: Thames and Hudson, 1982.

Dawson, Warren, and Eric Uphill. *Who Was Who in Egyptology: A Biographical Index of Egyptologists; of Travellers, Explorers and Excavators in Egypt; of Collectors of and Dealers in Egyptian Antiquities; of Consuls, Officials, Authors, Benefactors and Others, whose names occur in the Literature of Egyptology, from the year 1500 to the present day, but excluding persons now living.* London: Egypt Exploration Society, 1972.

Fagan, Brian. *The Rape of the Nile: Tomb Robbers, Tourists, and Archaeologists in Egypt.* New York: Scribner's Sons, 1975.

Gillispie, Charles Coulson, and Michel Dewachter, eds. *Monuments of Egypt: The Napoleonic Edition, The Complete Archaeological Plates from La Description de l'Égypte,* 2 vols. Princeton: Princeton Architectural Press, 1987.

Greener, Leslie. *The Discovery of Egypt.* New York: Viking Press, 1966.

Said, Edward. *Orientalism.* New York: Random House, 1978.

Stevens, MaryAnne, ed. *The Orientalists: Delacroix to Matisse, European Painters in North Africa and the Near East.* Exh. cat., London Royal Academy of Arts, 1984.

Nineteenth-Century Travel Accounts

Belzoni, Giovanni. *Narrative of the Operations and Recent Discoveries within the Pyramids, Temples, Tombs and Excavations in Egypt and Nubia.* London: Murray, 1820.

Edwards, Amelia. *A Thousand Miles Up The Nile.* New York: A.L. Burt & Co., 1888.

Flaubert, Gustave. *Flaubert in Egypt: A Sensibility on Tour.* Trans. and ed. by Francis Steegmuller. Chicago: Academy Chicago, 1979.

Gordon, Lucie Duff. *Letters from Egypt.* Revised edition with memoir by her daughter Janet Ross and introduction by George Meridith. New York and London: McClure, Phillips & Co. and R. Brimley Johnson, 1904.

Nightingale, Florence. *Letters from Egypt: A Journey on the Nile, 1849–1850.* Selected and introduced by Anthony Sattin. New York: Weidenfeld and Nicolson, 1987.

Twain, Mark. *The Innocents Abroad or the New Pilgrim's Progress: Being Some Account of the Steamship Quaker City's Pleasure Excursion to Europe and the Holy Land.* Hartford, Connecticut: American Publishing Company, 1869.

INDEX

A Thousand Miles up the Nile, 37–38
Abdullah Frères, 36, 40–41, 156
Abdul Kerim Fade, 29
Aboukir, 14, 154
Abu Simbel, 19, 21, 41, 154
Academies des Inscriptions et Belles-lettres, 28
Academies of Sciences and Fine Arts, 22
"Alastor; Or, the Spirit of Solitude", 20
Alexander the Great, 12–13
Alexandria, 30, 37, 39, 155
Amenhotep I, 41
Antiquities, 15
Antiquities Museum, 40, 155
Antony, Mark, 13
Arabian Nights, 20
Arago, François, 22, 24
Archer, Frederick Scott, 33, 34, 155
Army of the Nile, 11, 14, 17, 154
Around the World in Eighty Days, 155
Assuan, 30
Augustus, 13

Baring, Sir Evelyn, 155
Bartlett, W.H., 31–32
Battle of the Pyramids, 11, 12, 17
Bayard, Hippolyte, 25
Beato, Antonio, 36, 37, 156
Beato, Felix, 36–37, 156
Béchard, Henri, 43, 157
Bedford, Francis, 35, 36, 157
Belzoni, Giovanni, 19, 154
Benecke, E., 29, 157
Bernard the Wise, 16
Birch, Samuel, 25
Blanquet-Évard, 27, 28
Bonfils, Félix, 42
Bonfils, Adrien, 157
Bonfils, Marie-Lydie Cabanis, 157–58
Bonfils family, 36
Botta, Paul Émile, 37
Bouchard, François-Xavier, 22
Bouton, Charles, 23
Braun, Adolphe, 158
Brewster, Sir David, 155
Bridges, George, 28
British Museum, 19, 22, 25, 37, 154
Brugsch, Émile, 41, 155
Bulak, 28

Caesar, Julius, 13
Cairo Museum, 41
calotype, 20–21, 25, 26, 27–28, 34
Cammas, Henry, 158
Champollion, Jean François, 22, 27, 154
Cheops, King, 11, 38
Cleopatra, 20, 32, 41
Cleopatra's Needle, 37, 155
Commission de l'Égypte, 12, 15
Cook, Thomas, 12, 38–40, 155
Crimean War, 155
Crystal Palace Exhibition, 39

Daguerre, Louis-Jacques Mandé, 22–23, 24, 154
daguerrotype, 22–25, 154
Dar el-Bahri, 41
De Clercq, Louis, 20, 21, 158
Dean and Dawson, 40
Délié, Hippolyte and Émile Béchard, 36, 40, 159
Della Valle, Pietro, 16
Dendara, 38
Denon, Baron Dominique Vivant, 17–18, 154
Desaix, General, 17
Description de l'Égypte, 15–16, 22, 24, 27, 154
Dévéria, Théodule, 28
Diodorus Siculus, 13
Drovetti, Bernardo, 18
Du Camp, Maxime, 26–27, 28, 29, 32, 36, 41, 159

Edwards, Amelia, 37–38, 40, 43
Égypte, Nubie, Palestine et Syrie, 27
Égypte et Nubie, 27
Egyptian Exploration Fund, 34, 38, 155
Eugénie, Empress, 38
Excursions daguerriennes, 24

Flaubert, Gustave, 20, 26, 32, 41, 154
Fourier, Jean-Baptiste, 12–14, 15, 27
Franz Joseph, Emperor, 38
French Academy of Inscriptions, 27
French Expedition, 14, 16, 18
Frith, Francis, 30, 32–35, 36, 43, 159
Gaze and Son, 40
Gerôme, Jean-Léon, 42
Giza, 11, 24
Good, Frank Mason, 35, 159
Goodman, C.E., 158
Goupil-Fesquet, Frédéric, 23–24

Great Pyramid, 12
Greene, John Beasley, 20, 21, 24, 26, 28, 29, 36, 43, 160
Guide for Travellers in Egypt, 30, 31

Haight, Sarah, 30
Hammerschmidt, W., 37, 160
Herodotus, 16
hieroglyphics, 22, 24, 25, 154
Hogg's Polytechnic tours, 40
Holmes, Oliver Wendell, 37
Homer, 12
Horus, 17
Hugo, Victor, 19, 20, 26

Illustrated London News, 37
Imbaba, 11
Innocents Abroad, 155
Interior Colonnade at Edfu, 21
Island of Roda, 32

Jerusalem, 34
John Frame's Tours for Teetotallers, 40
Joly de Lotbinière, Pierre, 23–24

Karnak, 21, 23, 27
Khedive, 40, 41
Kingslake, Alexander, 26
Kodak, 155
Korosko, 27

Lake Nasser, 12
Lancet, Michel-Ange, 14
Layard, Austen, 37
Le Gray, Gustave, 25, 26, 28, 160
Le Nil, 28
Lear, Edward, 29–30
Lerebour, Nicolas, 24
"Les Orientales", 19, 26
Lesseps, Ferdinand, 155
Levi-Strauss, Claude, 11
Liverpool Photographic Society, 32
Louis Phillipe, 20
Louvre, 18
Luxor, 18, 36, 154
Lycurgus, 12

Mamelukes, 11, 16, 17, 19
Mariette, Auguste, 38, 40, 42, 155
Maspero, Gaston, 41
McDonald, Sergeant James, 161
Medinet-Habu, 24, 28, 29

Memphis, 23
Modern State, 15
Mohammed-Ali, 17, 19, 28, 154
Mokba, Sheik, 29
Moses, 32
Mosque of Sultan Quait-Bey, 36
Mount of Olives, 34
Murray, Robert, 28, 161
Murray, John, 154
Murray's Handbook, 40, 154

Napoleon, 11–15, 17, 22, 154
Napoleon III, 29
Naya, Carlo, 161
Nefertari, Queen, 41
Nelson, 14, 154
Nightingale, Florence, 32
Nubia, 26, 29

Osiris, 14
Ottoman Empire, 16, 17, 36
Ouenephes, 38
"Ozymandias", 9, 154

Palestine, 24, 26, 37
Panorama d'Égypte et de Nubie, 24
Pasha, Abbas, 154, 155
Pasha, Arabi, 155
Pasha, Halem, 29
Pasha, Ibrahim, 32, 154
Pasha, Ismail, 40, 155
Pasha, Said, 155,
Petrie, Sir Flinders, 38
Philae, 12, 14, 27, 29, 30, 34, 36
Place de Concorde, 18, 154
Plato, 12
Pliny, 16
Pompey, 13
Pompey's Pillar, 37
Prince of Wales, 35, 38, 39, 41
Princess of Wales, 38, 39
Pyramid of Chepran, 19
Pyramids, 11–12, 16, 34, 37
Pythagoras, 12

Ramses II, 19, 34, 41, 154
Reigate, 35
Roberts, David, 29, 33, 154
Robertson, James, 37, 161
Romanticism, 19–21, 24, 26
Rosetta, 22

Rosetta Stone, 22, 154
Rousseau, Louis, 29, 161
Rug Dealer, 42
Rug Merchant, 42
Ruskin, John, 35
Russell, William, 39

Sadad, Sheik, 42–43
Saint-Maur, Captain de Verminac, 18
Salt, Henry, 18, 19
Saqqara, 38
Schoefft, Otto, 162
Schranz, Anton, 162
Sebah, J. Pascal, 36, 162
Seti I, 19, 41
Shelley, Percy Bysshe, 19, 20, 154
Shepheard's Hotel, 39, 40
Smith, John Shaw, 28
Société Asiatique, 28
Société Orientale, 28
Solon, 12
South Midlands Temperance Association, 38, 39
Sphinx, 12, 41
Strabo, 14, 16
Suez Canal, 38, 40, 155

Talbot, William Henry Fox, 24–25
Talbotype Applied to Hieroglyphics, 25

Taylor, Baron Isidore, 24
Terry, Lt. Astley F., 37
Terry Album, 37
Teynard Félix, 16, 20, 24, 26, 27, 28, 29, 43, 155, 162
Thebes, 16, 19, 23, 30, 34, 40, 41
Thotmes II, 41
Thutmose III, 155
Tour du Monde, 36
Traveller's Handbook to Egypt, 154
Tremaux, Pierre, 29, 162–63
Tristes Tropiques, 11
Trojan War, 12
Turin, 18
Twain, Mark, 11, 155

Universal Exposition, 33, 39
University of Chicago, 155

Verne, Jules, 155
Vernet, Horace, 23, 24
Victoria, Queen, 35, 154
Views in the Holy Land, 33
Voyage dans la Basse et la Haute Égypte, 17–18, 154
Voyages pittoresques, 24

Wenham, Francis, 32-33
Wheelhouse, Lieutenant, 28

ABOUT THE AUTHORS

KATHLEEN STEWART HOWE

Kathleen Stewart Howe is a Ph.D. candidate in the History of Photography at the University of New Mexico. She was awarded the 1993–94 Chester Dale Fellowship from the Center for Advanced Study in the Visual Arts at the National Gallery of Art, Washington, D.C. She has also written *Felix Teynard: Calotypes of Egypt, A Catalogue Raisonné*, New York: Kraus, Hershkowitz, and Weston, 1992.

MICHAEL G. WILSON

Michael G. Wilson is a collector of nineteenth- and early twentieth-century photography. One of his major areas of interest is early travel and expedition photography in Egypt. When assembling his collection he was struck by the influence of tourism on photographic style. The investigation of this phenomena led to the exhibition *Travelers in an Antique Land: Early Travel Photography in Egypt* and this book.